HATCHET + BEAR

SPOON CARVING

EJ OSBORNE

PHOTOGRAPHY BY MARTE MARIE FORSBERG

quadrille

SPOON CARVING ESSENTIALS

SPOON CARVING SKILLS

SPOON CARVING PROJECTS

FOREWORD

The world of spoon carving has come a long way in the past few years. From the humble beginnings of perhaps only several dozen people in the UK who could carve a decent spoon, we now have a blossoming and rapidly growing spoon carving community.

There is something magical about being able to use simple hand tools to work green wood, straight from the tree, into useful objects for our daily lives. EJ Osborne has a unique way of expressing and sharing that magic through his website, Instagram feed, and now also this book. Through his sharing, a great many more folk are connecting with the natural world in a meaningful way and – just perhaps – helping us all towards a better future.

ROBIN WOOD MBE

Woodworker and founding chair of the Heritage Crafts Association

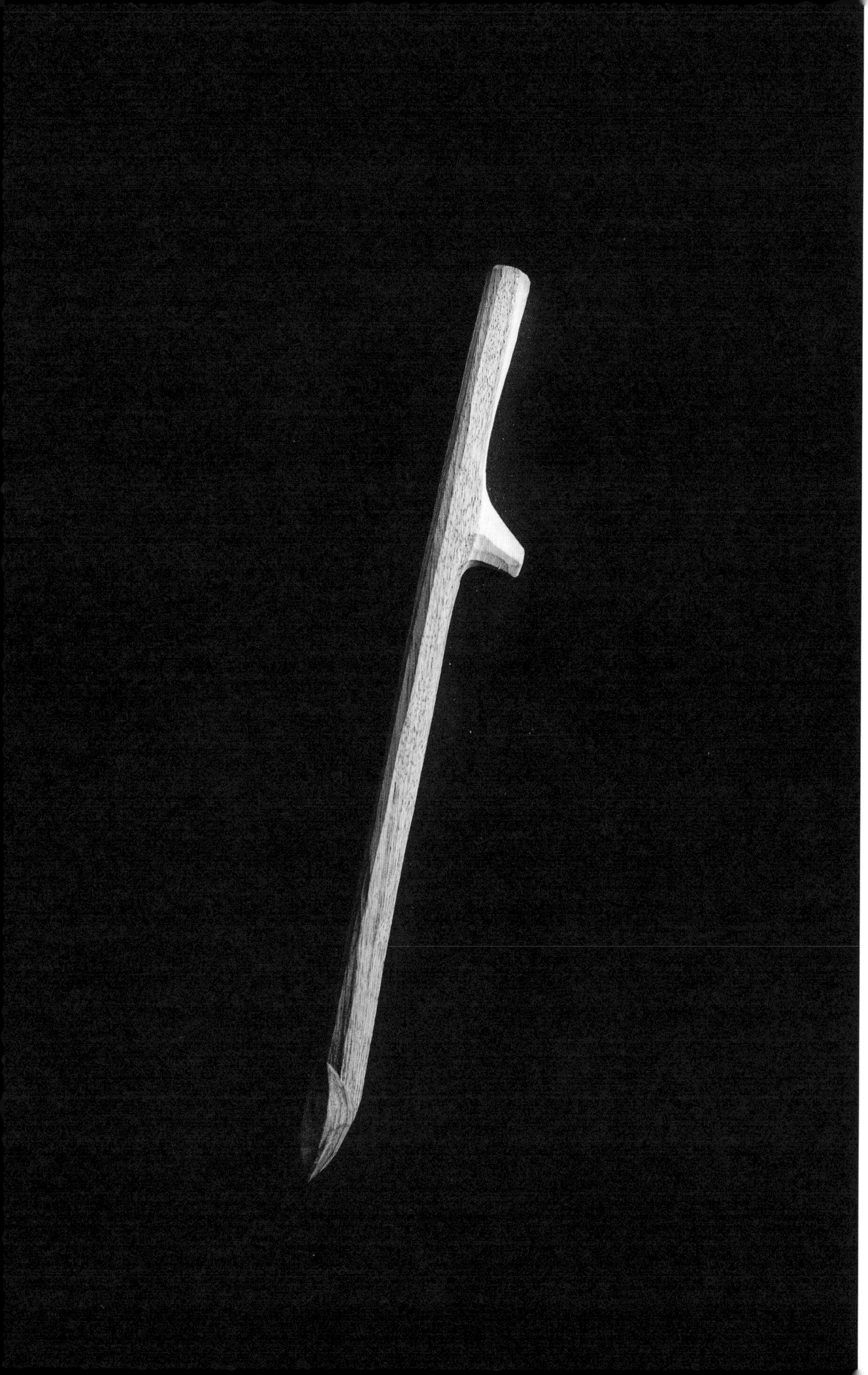

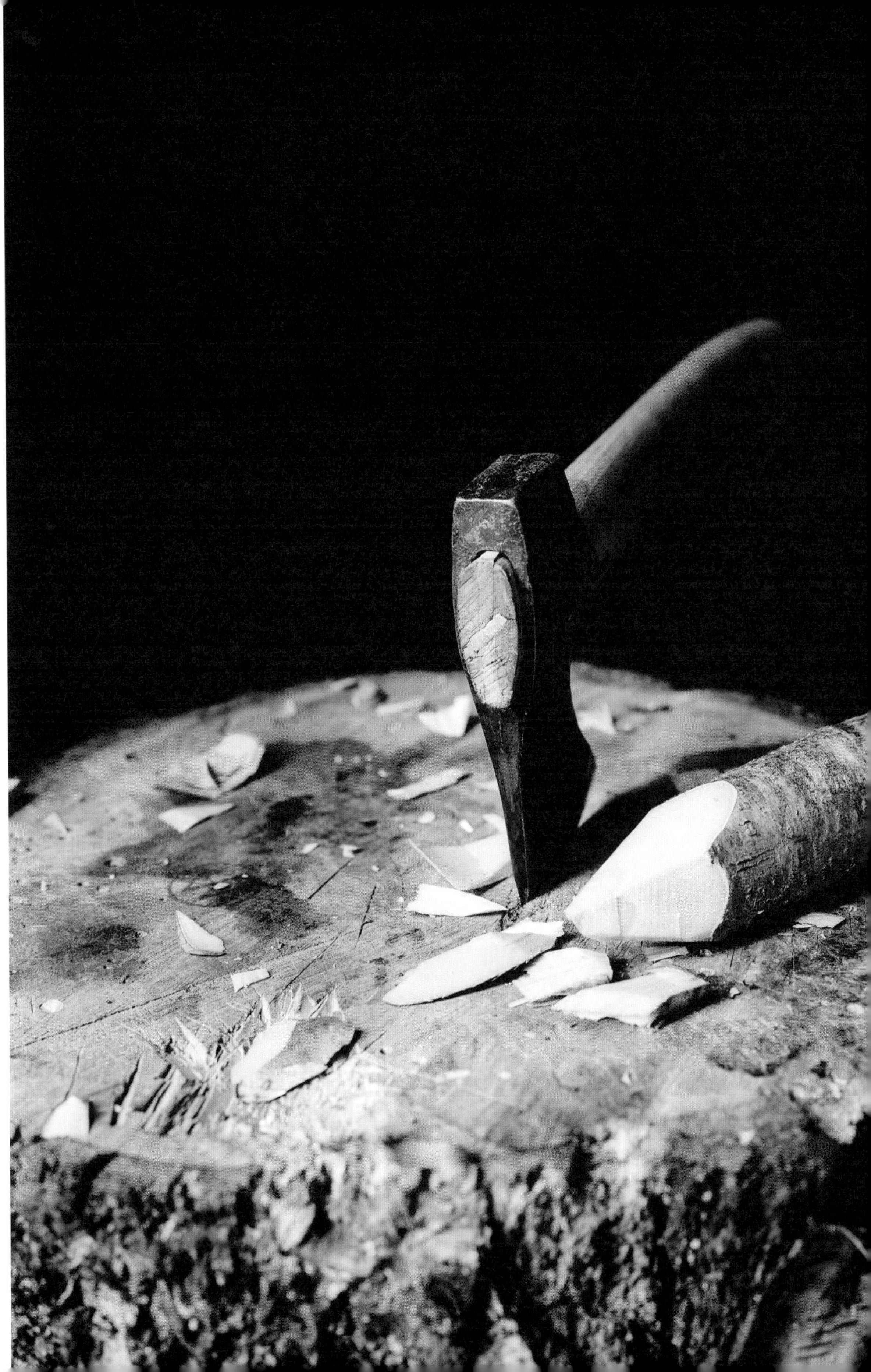

INTRODUCTION

Anyone can learn to carve a wooden spoon. And I believe everyone should. Spoon carving is one of those pastimes that, until you try it for yourself, you will never truly understand how this simple craft can enrich your life. Pairing my own joyful experience with the delight I have witnessed on the faces of others at the end of one of my spoon-carving workshops, I would go so far as to say that carving a wooden spoon is medicinal.

My spoon-carving journey started back in 2011. After studying Product and Furniture Design at university, I left my studies knowing that I did not want to sit in front of a screen all day, that I did not want to design objects for mass manufacture and – perhaps most importantly – that I did not want to be responsible for sending meaningless products out into an already overcrowded world.

While I knew exactly what it was that I did not want to do, I struggled to find the right direction in which to take my design career. So I took a break. During this time my partner and I moved out of urban London to rural Somerset and, at the same time, we started a family. Like most new parents, I was initially kept busy by all things baby and consequently distracted from my design-career dilemma. After my daughter's first eighteen months, the urge to create then started to creep back in.

When you are a creative or a maker but, for whatever reasons, you do not create or make for some length of time then you will eventually succumb to what I call 'The Maker's Itch'. Makers need to make. I needed to make. I needed to think, to dream, and to create something. And that something needed to be soulful and meaningful, as well as tangible and tactile. As soon as I felt the creative impulse beginning to return, I fell ill with the flu. Now, I am not claiming that the two are necessarily connected, but in my state of delirium caused by this fever, I had the sudden revelation that I needed to carve a wooden spoon from the branch of a tree.

This was not a slow, creeping realization. No, it was a light bulb moment. It was an instantaneous awakening, right then and there… albeit a slightly delirious one. I threw aside the sheets, hauled myself out of my bed and down into the kitchen where I picked up

a paring knife. I headed out into the garden, down the path towards the bonfire heap. From this tangled pile I dragged a half-burnt length of rhododendron branch onto the lawn. With that basic kitchen knife, I started to slice, chop and carve into the branch. In no time at all, I cut myself, slicing across my thumb. It was at this point that I was persuaded to return to the house and helped back into bed.

That is the story of how I came to be a woodworker. Perhaps that day, enveloped in fever, I answered a calling. Perhaps when the impulse to create is left unfulfilled for long enough then The Maker's Itch can cause you to be physically unwell. I soon recovered from both the flu and the cut. The healing power of carving wooden spoons is such that I have been carving spoons and honing my green woodworking skills ever since.

Carving spoons feels good. It feels so good, in fact, that I do it all the time. Alongside all sorts of other wooden utensils and objects, which are made using the same traditional tools and skills, I sell my handcarved spoons through various outlets, including my online shop. I have given a TEDtalk about carving spoons and write daily blog posts, which more often than not contain information about my time wandering about in the woods, making things from trees and a fair amount of photographs of wooden spoon. I also teach small groups of people how to carve their very own spoons at my spoon-carving workshops. I do all of this under the moniker of Hatchet+Bear.

Using just three simple hand tools – a small axe, a straight-edge knife and a crook knife – you can shape the small branch of a tree into a simple, functional and honest spoon. A spoon that is both charming and unique. It is that simple. Spoon carving is a craft that focuses one's thoughts and attention, while being both calming and soothing. The act of carving, peeling and shaving wood is both absorbing and meditative. As minutes seem to turn into hours within the blink of an eye, it is all about the joy of slow living.

Carving spoons can be done at any time of the day, in any place, alone or within a group. I hold my workshops in the middle of the woods, around an all-day campfire, with no more than ten people attending at any one time. Upon arrival, I often hear people apologetically claim 'I am not very creative,' or, 'I am rather clumsy,' but once the wood shavings start to fly, these are two things that turn out to be invariably untrue.

Once each spoon-carving workshop is under way, I am always delighted to find that most people simply cannot stop. They are driven to keep on whittling away, rather than break for a cup of coffee. They become entranced. They are transported elsewhere. When I find myself in such company, I always think how this is a very special state that can only be good for us: powerful, absorbing, satisfying, and soul nourishing. Naturally, after a full day of carving wood, it always makes sense when I hear students say, 'It is amazing to find something that has allowed me to forget about my problems and completely switch off.'

After attending one of my workshops, a large number of past students have carried on spoon carving. When I say 'after', I mean straightaway. Not 'one day soon' or 'in my next spare moment', but the very next day. What's more, these students have no intention of ever stopping carving. I receive letters, emails and messages on social media from spoon carvers the world over, telling me how making wooden spoons has changed their lives for the better, how the practice continues to contribute to their wellbeing, and, having now carved a succession of spoons, how their woodworking skills are advancing.

Wonky is wonderful. That is something I repeatedly say to students and is worth considering for just a moment. To alleviate any habitual patterns of thought born directly from

the need to perfect things, understand that you are using a natural tree branch to make a simple utensil. Or perhaps I should say, put aside any notions you have about trying to make your spoon perfect as the beauty of a hand-carved item, such as a spoon, is found within the imperfections. The bent, crooked, swirling, jaunty, oddly shaped stem of woody goodness that you are about to repurpose into a functional utensil embodies the relationship between you and the tree. There is your perfection, right there.

Woodworking skills are something to be practised and perfected, of course. Becoming comfortable with the way you hold your tools and body while carving, the efficiency of the cuts you make, their placement and how accomplished they become over time is key, as well as enjoying and appreciating working with the many beautiful pieces of tree you will be fortunate to come across. The process of spoon carving, from finding and selecting suitable woods, to splitting, preparing and refining those woods into shapes, is a beautiful journey alone and I, myself, have often stayed in that place for as long as possible: free from worry or fuss about where I am going, what I am making or where it will end. Just whittling for whittling's sake, down into a pile of shavings.

Spoon carving is an holistic experience that uses all of our senses. When we start practising how to handle spoon carving tools at workshops, the most often heard comments relate to the scent of carving wood. There really is nothing else to compare that smell. As we peel away long shavings of bark and chop out chunks of soft, wet wood fibre, after having just sawn off the young branches of the trees which surround us in abundance, the heavenly aroma of sweet sap is released from the wood and mingles with the scent of torn bark, crunched-up leaves and heavy moss.

Messy is wonderful. When we carve spoons in the woods, getting grubby clothes, soily hands and covering ourselves in small flying chips of wood is inevitably going to happen. For anyone in the group who has arrived from the corporate sterility of an office or the concrete surroundings of an inner city, as the group merrily begin to work away I often overhear that messy is a welcome state to be in. Likewise, if you choose to sit in your living room, after everyone else has gone to bed, and whittle the night away into the early hours – who me? – you will indeed cover yourself and the floor around you in wood shavings. Standing up at the end of a carving session, watching all the shavings tumble from your lap to join the others on the floor while you cradle your newly emerged spoon, is a freeing experience. As long as you sweep up before the household wakes, no one will know exactly how much of a glorious mess you made.

By the time you have worked your way through this book, you will have a fair amount of spoon-carving experience under your belt… and hopefully some lovely spoons to show for it. Of course, your first few spoons are going to be a little rough around the edges. But they will be yours. You made them and you will be able to use them, cook with them, eat with them, toss salads with them and serve big sloppy pots of casserole with them.

A short time after I started to carve spoons, I realized that I was able to make any type of spoon, ones that were better suited to my individual needs or the needs of others. Spoons with long handles and wide heads, an incredibly long jar spoon for an unusually slender olive jar, a thick-necked dough-stirring tool, a left-handed spoon, an acorn-sized scoop with a slender handle to reach all the way to the back of the oven for a friend who needed one for some inexplicable reason. The wooden utensils you make to fulfill your culinary visions will be limited only by the designs within your imagination. These thoughts lead me to re-evaluate how much care I was putting into the food I was eating and cooking for my family. If you pour your energy, heart, and soul into making beautiful wooden spoons to use in the home, they will undoubtedly inspire you to cook and eat well. Have fun making them and using them. Welcome to the spoon zone.

Spoon Carving Essentials

Only a few basic hand tools are needed to carve an almost infinite number of wooden spoons. Alongside these hand tools, the most important ingredient in the recipe for making a wooden spoon is the green wood itself. Over the next few pages, I will explain the basic information you need to know when identifying, harvesting and storing green wood, and the basic tools you will need to transform this wood into spoons.

GREEN WOOD

WHAT IS GREEN WOOD?

Green wood is wood that has been freshly harvested from the tree, just felled, recently cut, or newly pruned. Green wood is full of water and sap, which means it will be soft and pleasurable to carve with a knife. This is opposed to 'seasoned' wood, which is older and drier and, as a result, is much tougher and more difficult to work with.

As soon as wood is cut from the tree, it starts to dry out. While seasoned wood is ideal for firewood, where it needs to be dry so that it burns successfully on a fire, it is a total pain to carve a spoon out of. If you want to carve beautiful spoons using only three simple tools, it is important to be using fresh green wood.

WHAT TYPE OF GREEN WOOD DO I NEED?

The short answer to this question is that you can use wood from any hardwood tree species. Where I live in the south west of the UK, for example, there is a wonderful array of native British hardwoods that I use to carve spoons from. A few of the species I use for carving are Wild Cherry, Birch, English Walnut, Elm, Sycamore, Beech, Hawthorne, Hazel, Chestnut, and the various fruit woods, including apple, plum and pear. This is where your tree identification guide book (see page 29) will prove to be one of the most essential items in your spoon carving kit.

HOW LONG DOES WOOD STAY FRESH OR 'IN THE GREEN'?

That depends on a two factors: the tree from which the wood is harvested and how the wood is stored. The timber of each tree species has different properties; some trees have a high water content while the water content of other species is naturally much lower. How you cut your harvested wood and where you store it greatly affects its 'use by date'. A log left whole or 'in the round' stays fresher for longer than a log that is split into smaller sections (see pages 87–93). Similarly, a branch left in the shade on a cool winter's day stays fresher longer than a branch placed in the sun on a hot summer's day.

Much to my family's amusement, I am always tricking branches into staying fresh by wrapping them up in plastic bags and putting them in the refrigerator. Experiment and have fun learning what works for you. The best green wood knowledge comes from experimentation.

SPOON CARVING KIT LIST

Only a few hand tools are required for spoon carving, all of which are inexpensive and serviceable. The following list is all you will need.

SMALL AXE

An axe is a beautiful tool indeed. It is a true workhorse, capable of carrying out more than most people realize. For spoon and utensil carving, it is important to use the right kind of axe. I prefer the Gransfors Brüks Wildlife Hatchet; the slim, curved blade is a fine shape for carving, balanced by a nice, short handle, and its overall weight is good for constant chopping and slicing. Avoid axes with chunky, wide heads that are designed for splitting wood as these do not work so well for carving.

STRAIGHT-EDGE KNIFE

For carving spoons, a good straight-edge knife is a must. While it does need to be a wood carving knife, as opposed to any old knife from the kitchen drawer, it does not have to be expensive. Knives for carving wood should have a slim and shallow blade with a 'Scandi' ground edge. A blade with a Scandi grind allows you to carve closely to the surface of the wood with precision.

CROOK KNIFE

Simply put, a crook knife is a knife with a bent blade. It is used to scoop out hollows of varying depths from wood. In spoon carving, a crook knife is used to carve out the bowl of a spoon. Crook knives are made to be specifically left- or right-handed, so make sure you buy one that suits you. They also come in different sizes with a choice of curves. Some crook knives are tiny, for making utensils such as salt and spice scoops, while others are really big, for making objects like ladles and cups. I use a medium-sized crook knife for pretty much everything. It is a good all-rounder and can be used for making lots of different types and sizes of spoon bowls.

FOLDING SAW

A decent folding or retractable saw is necessary for harvesting tree branches for carving. I always keep one in the van with me, just in case I drive past a woody haul. You will be surprised at just how much material you can cut through with a saw blade that is only 15cm–20cm (6–8 in.) long. A well-made saw will stay sharp for a long time, plus the blades are often replaceable on the best ones.

LIFESYSTEMS
TREKKER
FIRST AID

BEETLE MALLET

A beetle mallet is a heavy duty tool used to tap the back of the axe head when splitting logs. The best ones are clubs made from tough hardwood and will last throughout years of constant use. It is easy to make your own beetle mallet from a piece of branch wood; I will show you how on pages 84–5.

CHOPPING BLOCK

A large section of tree trunk makes a useful chopping block when splitting wood and axing out rough shapes, or 'spoon blanks', as they are known before they are whittled into more identifiable spoon shapes. When selecting a tree trunk for a chopping block, pick one with a diameter of approximately 30cm (12 in.). Likewise, an average height of 40cm (16 in.) is a good size. Adjust the height measurements to suit your own requirements, but I find it is useful to have a chopping block that you can use while either sitting or standing. If a piece of wood with a large diameter has come your way, but it does not have enough height to make a viable chopping block, you can always put some legs on it to bring it up to the correct height. However, do bear in mind that the chopping block needs to be at least 20cm (8 in.) in depth to ensure it can take the impact of the axe without splitting in two itself. When cared for, a heavy-duty chopping block will last you for many years. Mine lives indoors.

GRAPHITE PENCIL

The best tool to use for drawing spoon designs and outlines onto wood is a simple graphite pencil. The best kind of graphite pencil for drawing onto fresh, moist, green wood is an indelible pencil, which has had a permanent coloured dye added to the graphite so that the marks it makes cannot be erased. Indelible pencils also go by the names of copy pencils and document pencils.

FIRST-AID KIT

The simple fact of the matter is that no one has learnt to carve wooden spoons without cutting a finger… or two. Keep a basic first-aid kit to hand, plus an extra box of standard-size, rectangular fabric plasters. I recommend fabric plasters because they stay in place for longer. After you have put a plaster over your cut, you will want to get straight back to carving your spoon. A cheap plastic plaster will work its way off almost immediately after you stick it on. If you do cut yourself, rinse the cut thoroughly under a running tap, place a clean fabric plaster over the wound and keep the cut clean.

TREE IDENTIFICATION GUIDE BOOK

I have lost count of the number of tree identification guide books I own. I have spent the past five years on a mission to collect every one that I see in order to determine which is the best one. I buy up an old tree identification guide book from thrift stores whenever I spot one, so by now I most definitely have duplicate copies. Suffice to say, my tree identification guide book collecting has become more of a habit as opposed to a necessity. I have a tree identification guide book problem. My main advice to you is to make sure that the guide book you purchase is specific to your continent, or preferably your country, and is the latest, most up-to-date edition available. Unless you want to learn about every tree species worldwide, it is better to focus on those trees growing near to you as these will supply the wood that you will be using to carve your spoons.

SHARPENING TOOLS

Three simple facts: the best-looking spoons are carved with sharp tools; the safest way to carve is with sharp tools; carving is easier and more pleasurable when using sharp tools. If you buy good quality tools they are likely to arrive sharp, but after having carved a few spoons, you will need to re-sharpen them. Sharpening tools is an enjoyable craft in its own right and once mastered, the simple techniques you are using to hone your axe, straight-edge knife and crook knife can be easily adapted to service all manner of things, from chisels to lawn mower blades. Spend time learning how to sharpen your tools well.

Spoon Carving Skills

Over the following pages, you will learn how to use the three main tools for spoon carving – the axe, the straight-edge knife and the crook knife. From this point onwards, it is advisable to follow the instructions given in this book in the order in which they are given. Each technique and project builds upon the preceding skill learnt, eventually providing you with a solid foundation in how to use your hand tools safely and efficiently.

USING A SMALL AXE

It is common for new woodworking students to feel a nervous about using an axe for the first time, but after some guidance they soon realize that there is nothing to worry about and start enjoying the feeling of effortlessly chopping and slicing through chunks of wood. With a little practice on a few pieces of scrap wood, you too will soon become confident in using your small axe. This confidence will lead to smoother, more efficient cuts being accomplished by your axe with ease and enjoyment. Refer to the Spoon Carving Kit List on page 26 to find out what type of axe you need. Once you have your small axe in your working hand, sit to one side of your chopping block. If you are right handed, sit with the chopping block on your right. If you are left handed, then your chopping block should be to your left. Sit upright and relax your shoulders. Carefully take the protective sheath off the axe head. Make friends with your axe. You are now ready to begin... While you are practising these new axe skills, remember to take frequent breaks; after each skill learnt or every twenty minutes is ideal. Your muscles are not yet used to being exercised in this way. In the beginning, things will ache – especially the next day – so take it easy.

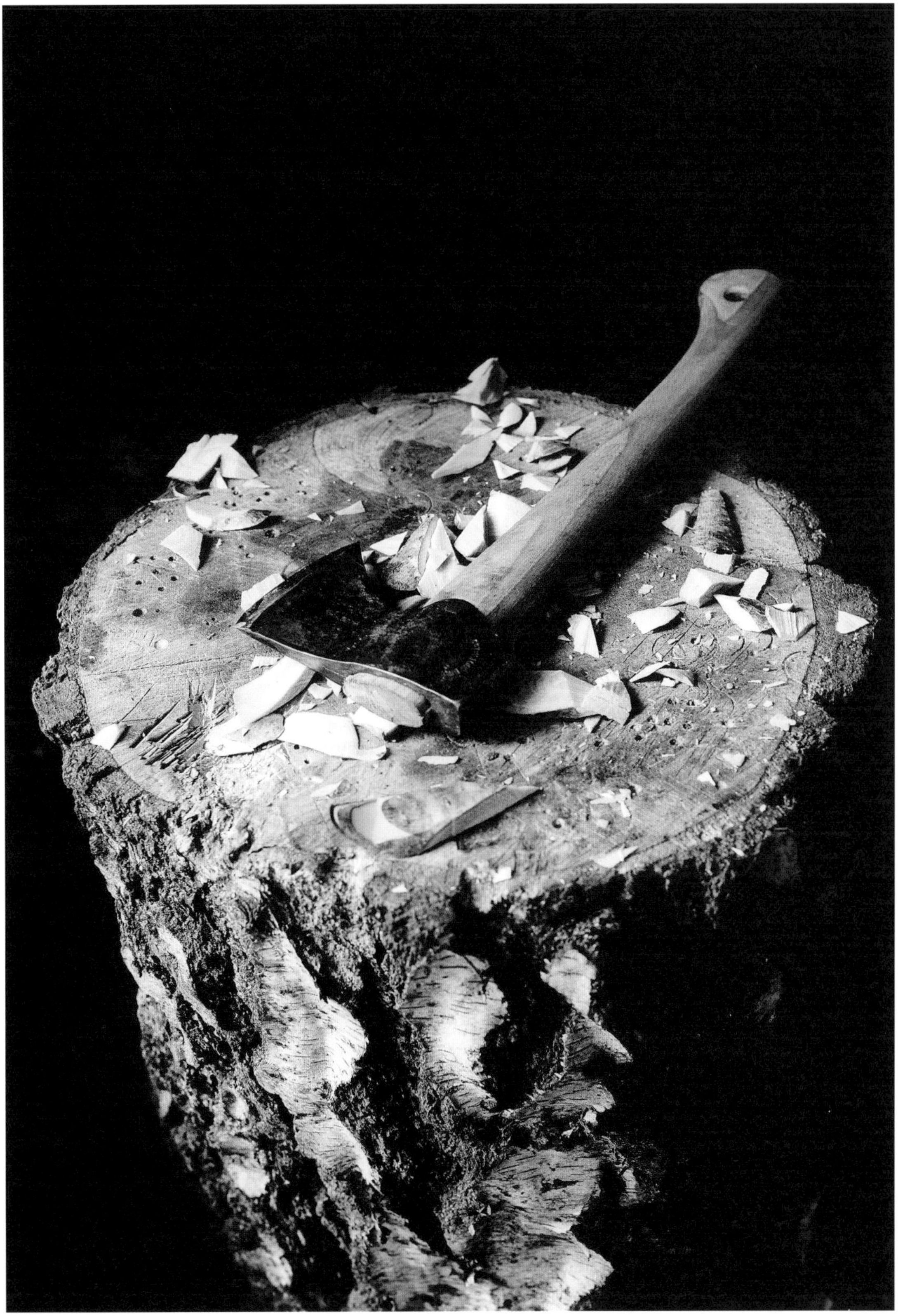

Chopping to a Point

This is a simple practice cut to hone your axe-handling skills. Basically, we are aiming to make a neat point on the end of a stick, much like sharpening a giant pencil. It will teach you how to carry out controlled and precise chopping with a small axe.

Take a length of branch wood between 3–5cm (1¼–2 in.) in diameter and about 50cm (20 in.) in length. Holding the axe in your working hand, assume the correct seated position to one side of your chopping block (see page 32). With your other hand, firmly hold the branch wood at the top of one end and place the other end towards the middle of your chopping block. Position the branch wood so it is roughly at a 45 degree angle to the surface of the chopping block. Grip the belly of the axe handle (the fattest part in the middle), making sure your thumb is fully wrapped around to meet your fingers and not resting on top of the handle.

Now, more than any other action, this cut is carried out most efficiently by bending your arm back and forth at the elbow. Make a point of 'chopping' the branch to remove slices of waste wood, rather than pushing or scrubbing the branch with the axe head. These are common mistakes I often witness with beginner spoon carvers at the start of each workshop. Flexing your arm at the elbow might seem like an awkward motion at first, but once you hit some sweet spots with your axe blade, you will begin to get a feel for the correct action. The waste wood should come off in flat pieces, leaving behind some relatively smooth facets on the branch.

When chopping, an axe generally performs at its best when it is moving up and down at a 90 degree angle to the chopping block. To ensure a 90 degree angle is maintained, the best approach is to keep the axe chopping up and down in the same place and to move the piece of wood instead, either by rotating the branch or changing its angle when you want to make a cut at another point on the wood.

Always keep your piece of wood towards the middle of the chopping block so that the blade of the axe finishes its cut safely away from the outer edge. Do not let the axe creep out to the edge. Similarly, never wrestle with a stuck axe. If a cut goes too deep and your axe blade gets stuck in the wood, stop, then gently leaver the axe head to the side before pulling it out from the wood.

Remember, chopping with an axe is not about speed. Work slowly at first, always with a relaxed and considered pace, and you will eventually find your chopping rhythm.

Once you have achieved a carved pencil point at one end of your branch, you can turn the piece of wood around and practise carving another point at the other end. After plenty of practice, you will have enough pointed sticks to deal with a vampire invasion, otherwise they can be put to use in the garden or on the allotment as stakes or supports.

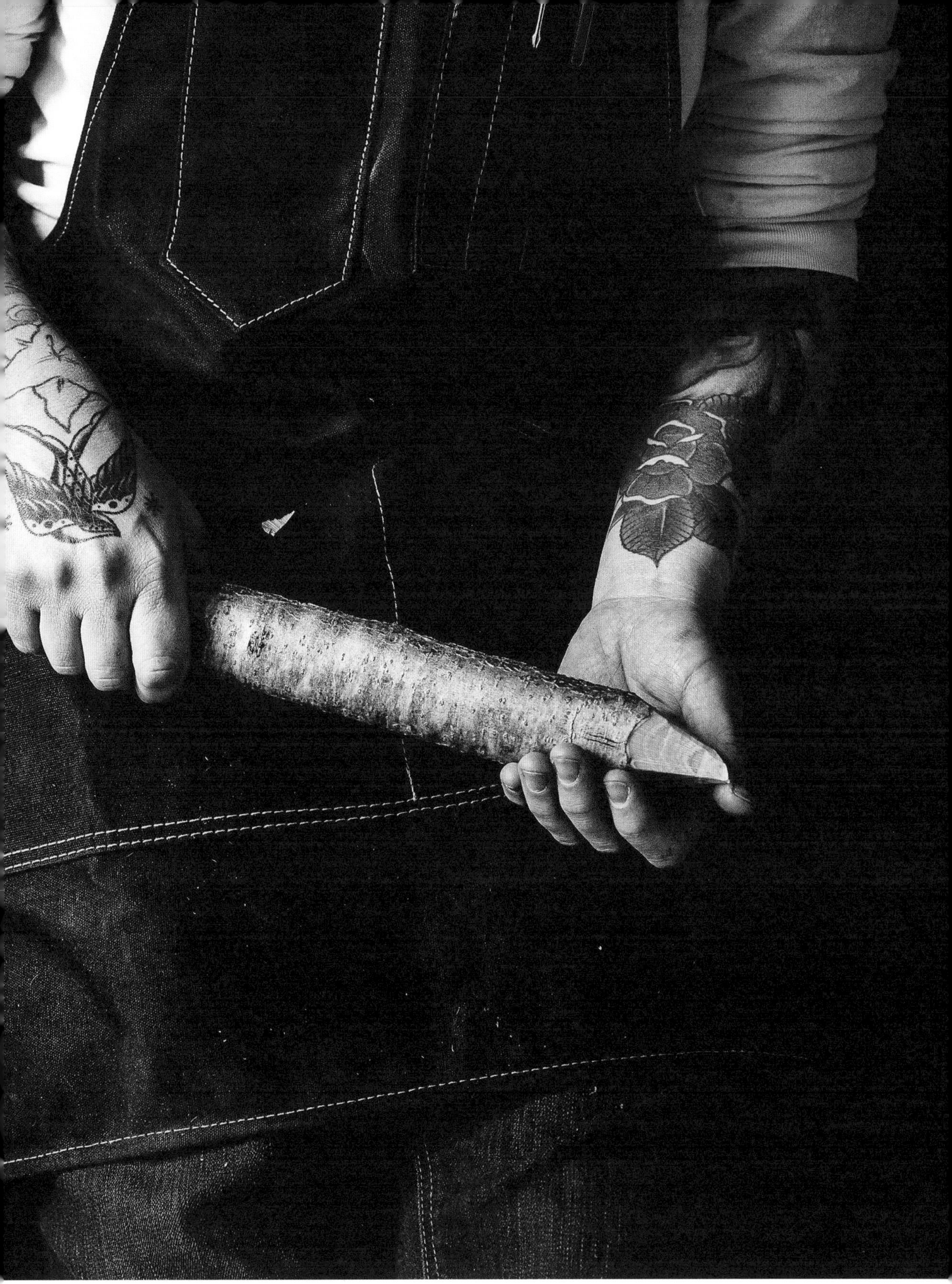

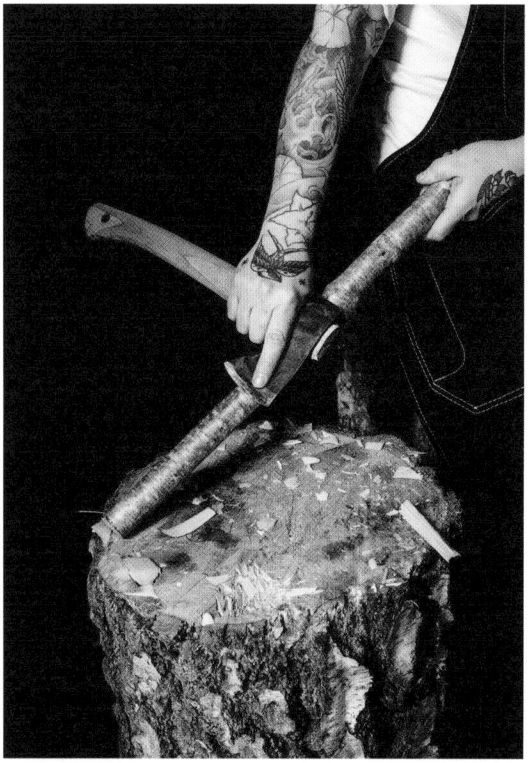

Planing Cut

This is a pleasurable cut in which the small axe is turned into a planing tool and then used to peel or shave bark from a branch or long piece of wood.

Holding the axe in your working hand, assume the correct seated position to one side of your chopping block as before (see page 32), but a little further away this time. Take another length of branch wood and, holding it firmly at the top of one end, place the other end towards the middle of your chopping block. Again, angle the wood so it is roughly 45 degrees to the surface of the chopping block.

Grip the axe as far up the handle as close to the axe head as possible. Take your first finger and place it straight across the flat cheek of the axe head, but making sure the tip of your finger does not overlap the sharp blade of the axe.

The power of this planing cut comes from the shoulder, as opposed to the elbow, so the action of this cut is very different to the one used for chopping wood. Keeping your arm straight and elbow locked, place the axe head flat against the wood near the bottom of the branch (or chopping block end). Drag the axe head up the length of the branch while raising your shoulder up towards your ear. Never take the blade of the axe above your hand that is holding the branch wood.

Once the axe has been dragged up the branch through raising your shoulder, tilt the edge of the blade very slightly inwards – just enough to register it against the bark – and then slowly push the axe blade back down the branch, all the way to the bottom. Keep your arm locked straight the whole time. Make sure that you finish this planing cut towards the middle of your chopping block. To continue shaving further strips of bark from the wood, rotate the branch and repeat this planing cut.

If there are any sizeable knots in the branch wood, they will definitely halt you in your tracks. For now, just work this planing cut up to any knots, stop, and then move on to another section of wood. Remember, never wrestle with the axe. Similarly, if you go too deep with this cut then stop, lever the blade to the side, then gently taking it out of the branch.

It will take a few practice goes of this planing cut to achieve one long peel of bark, but when you do, it so satisfying that you will want to repeat this cut endlessly.

Release Cut

The Release Cut is a useful cut that enables you to chop and carve away sections of wood while, at the same time, controlling where the axe stops cutting and how much wood it removes. As well as a Release Cut, it is also known as a Stop Cut or Relief Cut.

Sitting at the chopping block in the same position as before (see page 32), hold a length of branch wood (no less than about 40cm or 16 in. long) at one end. Rest the other end of the branch on your chopping block towards the middle. With your working hand, grip the axe around the handle at its belly, just as you did when you were chopping giant pencil points (see page 34).

Holding the wood at a 45 degree angle to the chopping block and, starting at the bottom of the branch, make a single chopping cut into the side of the branch to leave a short angled cut. Make another chopping cut about 10cm (4 in.) higher than the first and then continue to make more identical cuts at 10cm (4 in.) intervals stopping when you reach about two thirds of the way up the length of wood. Remember, never raise the axe blade higher than the hand that is holding the piece of wood.

You should find that the axe blade will chop easily into the wood, but do not worry as it will not chop all the way through the branch. This is because you are chopping against the wood grain, rather than with it. I will talk more about wood grain, as we progress through this book.

Once you have made the last and highest Release Cut, change the angle of the branch so it is almost vertical and carefully chop back down the length of the branch wood to remove material. Every time the axe blade hits one of the evenly spaced Release Cuts, a controlled piece of wood will fall away. Had you not made these initial Release Cuts and simply started to carve long strips of wood from the top to the bottom of the branch, then you would have run the risk of the axe splitting the wood rather than cutting it.

Once you have removed the wood all the way down the length of the branch, you can either make another set of Release Cuts on the same path – thereby allowing you to carve deeper – or you can rotate the piece of wood and start a new path of Release Cuts.

When you are finished for the day, give the axe blade a gentle wipe and put it back in its sheath. If you have been using your axe outside, bring it indoors into the warm and dry as it will not like being left out in the damp or rain. Take a moment to look around you and marvel at all the wood chipping and shavings, before moving on to learn some knife skills.

“

Spoon carving is about working with the natural grain of the wood, rather than imposing an ‘ideal’ shape onto it. When the need to strive for perfection melts away, then you are free to enjoy the making process.

”

USING A STRAIGHT-EDGE KNIFE

Over the following pages, I will show you how to use a straight-edge knife. We will concentrate on learning and practising eight of the most common knife skills used in spoon carving. Some knife skills can feel a little awkward at first. This is because most of us only ever use a knife to slice bread or to chop fruit and vegetables. When spoon carving, the grip, action and direction of a knife is much more varied. So relax, and try not to get too frustrated. It will all come to you in good time. But do make sure you are using a sharp straight-edge knife. The great thing about the knife skills you are about to learn is that they need not be limited to carving spoons. Once you are on your way to mastering these cuts, you will find they are brilliant for carving lots of other objects too.

Push Cut

When teaching straight-edge knife skills, I always show my students how to achieve this particular Push Cut first. Being the most basic of all the knife cuts, it allows you the time and space to get used to handling your knife, as well as learning some basic knife safety.

Take a length of wood (again about 50cm (20 in.) long). If using branch wood, it should be roughly between 2–3cm (1–1½ in.) in diameter. Making sure that your thumb is wrapped around the knife handle to meet your fingers (see overleaf) and not resting on the top of the knife blade, hold your knife using this standard grip with the blade facing downwards. Sitting facing forwards and with a straight back, hold the length of wood towards the top end. Bring the wood all the way over your legs, as far as your holding arm can comfortably stretch across your body, on to the same side as your working hand holding the knife and so that your forearm, wrist or knuckles are resting on your outer thigh. Avoid resting the piece of wood on your leg at any time.

The power of this Push Cut comes from the shoulder, just as it does when working the Planing Cut with the small axe (see page 39). With a straight arm, place the knife blade against the length of wood and, keeping your arm straight and elbow locked, drag the blade up the wood by raising your shoulder up towards your ear as far as it will go. As mentioned before when discussing the Planing Cut with the small axe, never take the blade above the hand that is holding the length of wood.

Register the knife blade against the surface of the wood as near to the handle end as possible. You get so much more power out of a cut when using the central belly of the blade, rather than the tip of the blade. Tilting the knife upwards slightly, and keeping your arm straight the whole time, slowly and steadily push the knife all the way down the length of wood.

If you go too deep with the Push Cut, inevitably the blade will get stuck. Do not wrestle with either the knife or the wood to release the blade. In a similar fashion to releasing a stuck axe, gently leaver the knife out to the side of the wood and then remove it. You can then peel off the offending piece of wood and start the cut again elsewhere.

With the Push Cut, you are aiming for a consistency of depth throughout the cut. Once you have practised this cut to the point of being able to achieve even consistency with your depth, you will then be able to shave some rather pleasurable lengths of wood from one place to another.

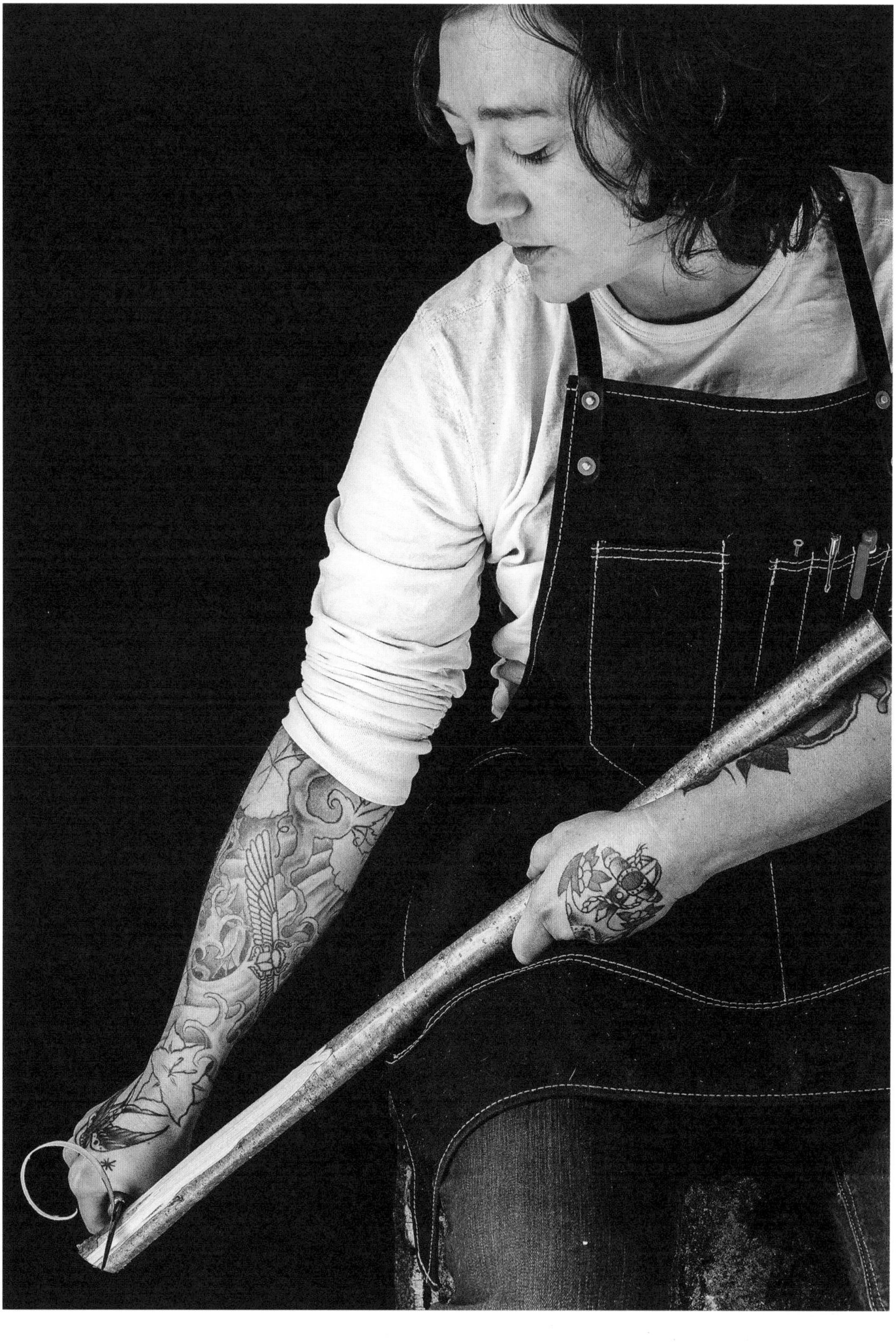

USING A STRAIGHT-EDGE KNIFE: PUSH CUT

Pull Cut

When I tell spoon carving students that they will be making a cut while pulling the blade towards themselves, this Pull Cut is the one that everyone worries about the most. From a very early age, we are told to cut away from ourselves at all times. When executed correctly within spoon carving, the Pull Cut is a safe and incredibly efficient cut that is carried out while moving the knife blade towards you. This is the cut that will define you as a bona fide spoon carver. This is the cut that will elevate your carving into beautiful spoons, as opposed to average ones.

Rather than worrying about this cut, take both time and care when reading the following instructions. If you are ever in doubt when making any of the cuts used within spoon carving, simply mime the cutting actions before you execute them for real. This is the wonderful thing about using hand tools. I recommend that you mime this Pull Cut first, so you can see that there really is nothing to worry about.

Take another length of wood and, holding the top of one end in your hand, place the other end of the branch wood onto your sternum, or breast bone, so that the branch is positioned horizontally. Holding the knife using the standard grip as before (see page 50), but this time with the blade facing upwards and the tip of the blade pointing away from you, bring the knife up and place the blade onto the piece of wood. Start this cut just below the point where you are holding the wood with your other hand; never above, always below.

From a safety perspective, the three most important aspects when executing this cut are as follows: firstly, the knife is tilted forwards so that the tip of the blade is pointing away from you; secondly, when you pull the knife towards your body, the first and only thing that will make contact with your chest is the heel of your hand or inside of your wrist; lastly, that you keep your upper body in an upright position, with a straight back, so you do not lean your face too close into your work.

Mime the Pull Cut several times to make sure those three things are happening. Once you are comfortable with mimed action of the cut, then you can progress to making the cut for real.

You will notice that you cannot take the Pull Cut right to the bottom of the branch wood because the heel of your hand will prevent this. To complete the cut, turn the piece of wood around and finish with a Push Cut (see page 50).

As well as using the standard knife grip, you can also carry out the Pull Cut with an adjusted thumb position, moving it from the wraparound position to the opposite side of the handle and resting it on you first finger's knuckle (see opposite). Some people find this grip more comfortable.

Planing Pull Cut

The Planing Pull Cut is a variation on the Pull Cut (see page 55). They both make exactly the same kind of cut, but the Planing Pull Cut gives you a little more control. Later on, when you move onto the projects in this book, you will be able to pair the Planing Pull Cut with the Pull Cut to carry out a combination of spoon carving moves.

The most important aspect to understand about the Planing Pull Cut is that you need to make both of your hands work together in tandem. Begin by setting yourself up as you did for the Pull Cut with a similar length of wood and in exactly the same seated position, using the same posture, grip and safety precautions. You might like to use the adjusted thumb position (see page 55).

Before you make the Planing Pull Cut, unfurl the fingers of your hand holding the piece of wood into a slightly cupped position. Next, move your hand holding the knife so that it nestles into the backs of those fingers forming the cupped hand. This is where your hands will need to work together, and stay together, for the entirety of the cut. The grip of your wood-holding hand needs to be relaxed enough to slide freely down the length of the wood with the cut, all the while holding and supporting the cradled fingers of your knife-holding hand.

Register the knife blade against the wood. As with the Pull Cut, make sure that the knife is angled so the tip of the blade is pointing away from you and the heel of your knife-holding hand will be the first and only thing to make contact with your body when you finish the cut.

Gently pull the blade along the branch with the knife-holding hand and follow by pushing simultaneously with the wood-holding hand. Make sure the fleshy part of your thumb that is holding the branch wood is not too exposed: as you slide down the wood making the Planing Pull Cut, your thumb will be the part of you that is nearest to the knife blade.

Once you are able to achieve some nice long peels of wood without your hands separating from one another, you have mastered the Planing Pull Cut.

ANCHORED PULL CUT

The Anchored Pull Cut uses the same hand grips and positioning as the Planing Pull Cut but your wood-holding hand stays held in place while your knife-holding hand pivots at the wrist. The action used here is not so much a 'pull' with your cutting hand, but rather a 'push' with your wood-holding hand. Your hands must stay anchored together and work in unison the whole time. When practising the projects given later on in this book, the Anchored Pull Cut will be used to carve the necks and shoulders of spoons.

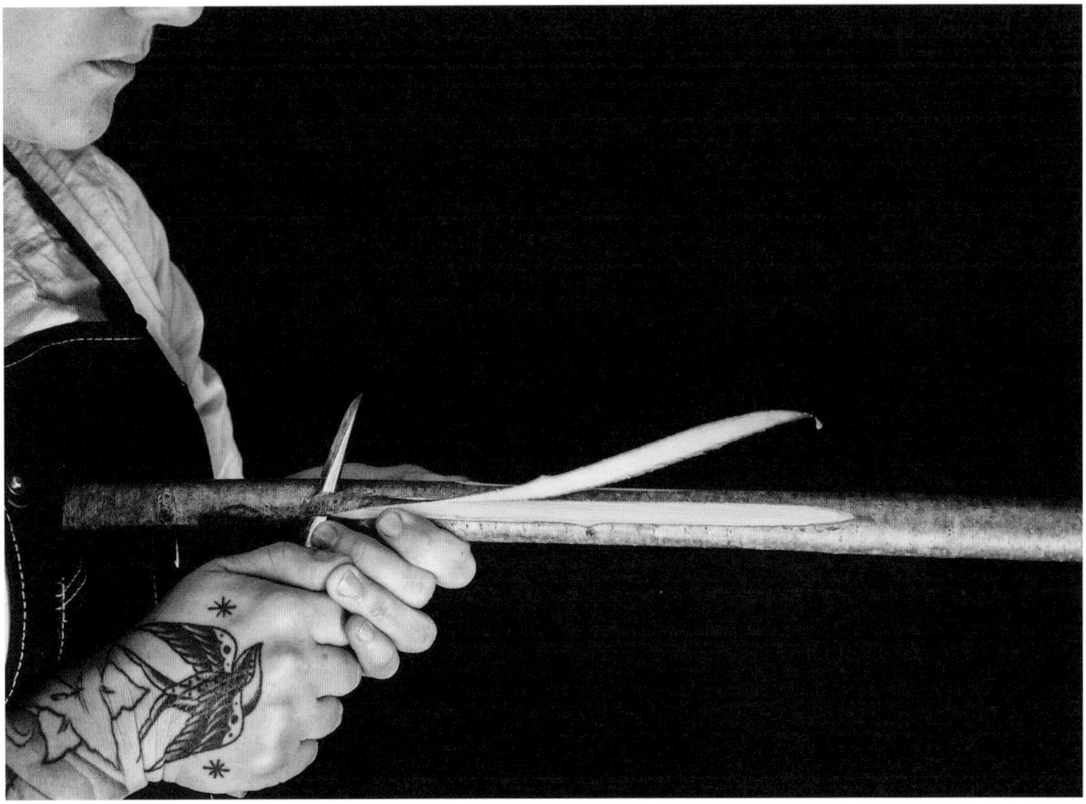

Potato Peeler Cut

I call this particular cut the Potato Peeler Cut because it reminds me of the action used to peel potatoes with a knife. It is a cut that works very well on small areas of material, as opposed to the more dramatic peels, slices and shavings you have been making up until now. Nonetheless, the Potato Peeler Cut is a very useful cut that can be used either to work down a length of wood or around a branch, so it is especially useful for nipping unwanted nubs off the ends of handles and fine finishing spoons. In this case, we are going to make this cut on the end of a branch to chamfer off the edges.

Again, the knife hold for this cut is the same as the previous two cuts: a wraparound grip with the blade facing upwards (see page 50). Bring your knife up to the wood. Adjust your grip by moving the thumb of your knife-holding hand off of the handle and anchoring it onto the very end of the piece of wood. Place the knife blade against the wood where you would like to make the cut, then mime executing the Potato Peeler Cut by drawing your fingers in and down the length of the branch so that the blade is moving towards you.

There are two things that you will need to make sure of when carrying out this mime: firstly, that your anchored thumb is positioned far enough down the branch away from the edge so that it is not in the path of the blade as you finish the cut; secondly, that your anchored thumb stays in place on the end of the branch wood after the cut is finished so that it does not ping away from the wood with the final motion of the cut.

This Potato Peeler Cut can be used to gouge quite deeply into the wood or it can be used to shave off the smallest of shallow slithers. Try practising both.

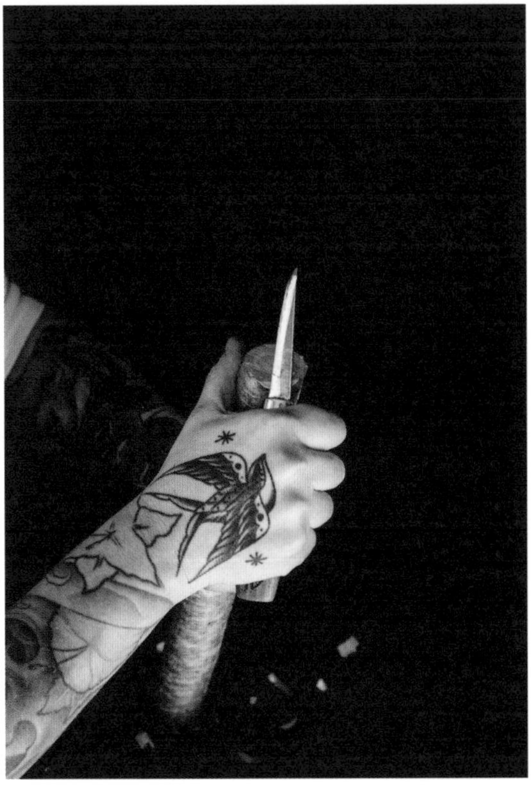

THUMB PUSH CUT

Like the Potato Peeler Cut, the Thumb Push Cut is another cut in which the stroke of the knife blade is limited to a small area. This cut has quite a wide variety of uses, such as making small chamfers on the ends of handles, creating small points and even sharpening your woodworking pencils, so it is well worth knowing.

As with the Potato Peeler Cut, you will be doing some more anchoring with your hands. With the blade facing down this time, hold the knife in a simple standard grip again in your working hand (see page 50). Hold a length of wood in your other hand (any piece of green wood will do). To practise this cut, cross the hand holding the knife over the top of the hand holding the branch. Register the knife blade on the wood where you want to make the cut. Next, take the thumb of your wood-holding hand off the piece of wood and place it onto the back of the knife handle. Make sure your thumb does not leave this position on the handle for the entirety of the cut. Even when the Thumb Push Cut is finished and the wood shaving has flown off, your thumb should still be anchored on to the knife handle.

With the edge of the knife blade against the wood and the thumb anchor acting as a pivot point, move the blade in a scissor-like motion to make the Thumb Push Cut. You should be flexing the wrist of your knife-holding hand to aid making the cut. It is like turning your hands and the knife blade into a pair of shears.

Chest Expander Cut

The Chest Expander Cut is my all-time favourite cut. It is the single cut that I use the most when carving spoons. Amazingly versatile, it can be used to make lots of different types of cuts in many different places on a spoon.

Some of my students take to this cut straightaway, while others need more time to click with it and find that all-important sweet spot. However, everyone agrees eventually that the Chest Expander Cut is a rather good move to master.

Any length of wood will do for practising this cut, but it is easier to start with something similar to the first few cuts we learnt – a longish length of branch wood with a small diameter.

Hold your knife so that the blade is facing upwards. Then, in the other hand, hold the length of wood at one end and tuck the other end under your armpit so that is heading backwards. Bring both fists upwards and inwards towards your body and rest your knuckles on your rib cage. The knife blade should now be facing outwards. For maximum control, leverage and safety, make sure your knuckles remain anchored to your rib cage for the entirety of the cut, just as we have done in previous cuts requiring anchor points. Register the blade onto the wood and then make the cut by working the knife blade down the length of the branch.

As I mentioned before, this is an extremely versatile cut, so you will be able to practise it in many ways. Firstly, try lopping off only small pieces of bark from the end of your branch. Once you have mastered this, try peeling longer pieces off the length of the wood. To do this you will need to adapt your technique a little into something called The Reverse Chest Expander Cut.

REVERSE CHEST EXPANDER CUT

Starting with your hands in exactly the same position as for the Chest Expander Cut, register the blade onto the wood. Keeping the knuckles of your knife-holding hand anchored to your rib cage, make the cut only this time, instead of keeping your wood-holding hand anchored as you did for the Chest Expander Cut, begin to pull it backwards. Make sure you keep the knife in the same spot and that you are actually moving the wood backwards to make the cut.

A useful tip with this cut is to use the side of your body as a brace for your wood-holding hand as you move it backwards. Hopefully by now, you will understand how using bracing areas and anchoring points when using a knife are really good working practices to adopt. They are essential in gaining optimum control, power and safety when carving and whittling.

It does not matter if you are not completely proficient in all the cuts I have shown you so far. Feel free to move on to the next section and learn how to use a crook knife. You can always return to brush up on your straight-edge knife skills later by practising and honing these techniques further.

When you have finished using your straight-edge knife, carefully and gently wipe the knife's blade with a dry cloth and store it safely.

“

If you pour your time, energy, and soul into hand carving wooden spoons to use within the home, they will undoubtedly inspire you to consider more carefully what you are cooking and eating.

”

USING A CROOK KNIFE

Over the following pages I will show you how to use a crook knife. Some people call this tool a spoon knife, a bent knife or a hook knife. Most commonly I refer to it as a crook knife due to the shape of the blade. When you start out carving, you can use any size, length or radius of blade you prefer. Take a look at the Spoon Carving Kit List for more information about the crook knife (see page 27). The following three crook knife skills I am going to teach you are all you need to learn in order to carve small, smooth spoon bowls into wood. As the bowl is what defines a spoon, these are crucial techniques to learn because they will enable you to transform pieces of wood into bona fide spoons.

Side-to-Side Cut

When hollowing out a piece of wood with a crook knife in order to shape a spoon bowl, it is always best to begin using a side-to-side action. The Side-to-Side Cut is the easiest way to gouge out material while shaping the basic foundations of a bowl. Take a piece of wood with a flat surface of no more than 5cm (2 in.) in diameter; a section of branch wood is a good choice. If necessary, using the axe skills you have already learnt (see pages 32–45) chop out a flat surface to work on.

Using an indelible pencil, draw a circle onto the flat surface of the wood. The circle can be any size but make sure that there are no knots within this area of wood. It is best to keep knots out of practice carving as much as possible as they can be rock hard and a tricky to work past.

Using the standard knife grip (see page 50), hold the crook knife so that the blade is curving upwards. Rest your knuckles on the piece of wood and then take your thumb away from the knife handle and place it on the side of the piece of wood. It is really important that your thumb is anchored in such a way that is below the flat surface of the wood and not on or protruding over the edge. Keeping your thumb anchored in place at all times, mime extending your fingers outwards while holding the handle and then drawing them back in again. This is the motion of the cut you will be making. After you have practised this action several times, you will be ready to attempt the cut.

Press with your anchored thumb, while unfurling your fingers out and then back in again. Aiming for the middle of the pencil circle, make a shallow gouge with the crook knife blade in the flat surface of the wood. Do not try to make the cut all the way from one side of the circle to the other.

In the past, I have found that at first some students will scrape the surface of the wood, as opposed to cutting it. If this is the case, it is just a question of adjusting the angle of the blade slightly and finding the sweet spot. Likewise, if you are not managing to make contact between the cutting edge of the blade and the surface of the wood, a slight adjustment will need to be made. Go easy. Remember, no wrestling.

I will say this again: make sure that your thumb rests below the surface of the wood at all times. As you probably realized when miming this cut, the blade of the crook knife will travel past the edge of the wood on its way to finishing the cut. You do not want the blade to end up in your thumb.

For this cut to work well, you need to work squarely across the wood fibres. As you will have undoubtedly already experienced while making your way through the practice cuts in the section of this book, the fibres within wood – the 'grain' – run vertically up and down its length. With the Side-to-Side Cut, you are working horizontally across the grain. At this stage, do not be tempted to try to cut vertically or diagonally. It will not work very well; you will end up wrestling with the blade, loosing control and cutting yourself.

Once you have made a few successful Side-to-Side Cuts in the middle of the pencil circle, start to extend the cuts a little further out, making the hollow larger. Slide your thumb up and down the side of the wood, anchoring at various points in order to carve further up or further down.

If you need to – and you probably will – you can turn the piece of wood around and cross your hands over to enable you to cut where you previously could not reach. Just make sure that when you do turn the piece of wood around and cross your hands, you then proceed to make the cut in exactly the same manner as before.

A valuable piece of advice for this cut is not to gouge too deeply, before moving on to extend the cuts. The cuts can be made to any depth you like, but try to keep the working area an even depth. The aim is to gouge the whole of the circle out. Practise this cut on different size circles and to different depths.

For the moment, the pencil circle you drew is just a guide. Try not to worry about the cleanliness of your outer circle too much at this stage. I will be showing you how to create clean curved edges later on.

For now, give your hands a rest and shake them out occasionally. They have been working hard.

USING A CROOK KNIFE: SIDE-TO-SIDE CUT

Down Cut

The Down Cut works in a similar way to the Side-To-Side Cut, in that you are making the same kind of gouging cut into the surface of the wood. However, as you are carving the grain vertically this time, the grip position for both hands will change. As it is very difficult to start this particular cut on a flat surface, it is best to practise this cut on a shallow hollow that you have created using the Side-to-Side Cut.

Grip the crook knife in your hand, again with the blade curving upwards, then take your thumb from the bottom of the handle and place it on top of the handle, next to your first finger. Hold the piece of wood as shown, cupping your fingers around the knuckles of your knife-holding hand. Once in position, mime this cut by flexing the wrist and rolling the knuckles of your knife-holding hand and allowing the blade to move in a gouging motion. You are aiming to keep your hands working together in tandem at all times; do not let them detach. They should still working in unison even when the blade of the crook knife has finished cutting.

This Down Cut is powered by the fingers of the cupped hand gently pushing the knuckles of the knife-holding hand as it rolls through making the cut. When you are happy with this motion, position the blade – this time on the edge of the pencil circle – and make the cut.

You will soon discover that you are only able to go downhill to the bottom or middle of your hollow. It is absolutely impossible to carry on carving uphill to the other side of the spoon bowl. Welcome to the first lesson in the laws of wood grain and its restrictions: you cannot carve uphill, no matter how hard you try.

You will need to turn the piece of wood around and, with exactly the same technique, make the downhill cut again. Stop at the bottom of the hollow to meet up with your previous Down Cut.

Because the wood grain runs vertically, this Down Cut is best achieved when the blade is positioned at 12 o'clock and 6 o'clock on the edge of the pencil circle. I suggest carving a few shallow hollows with the Side-To-Side Cut before moving on to practise the Down Cut.

USING A CROOK KNIFE: DOWN CUT

Curved Cut

This is the cut that will enable you to achieve crisp, sharp lines around the inside edge of your hollowed-out spoon bowl. When we move on to carving spoons in the project section, mastering this cut will make your spoon bowls look beautifully smooth, neat and tidy. No matter how well you master the technique, this Curved Cut will only give you the desired results when paired with a sharp crook knife.

As with most things in life, there are a few different ways in which tidying the edges of a spoon bowl can be carried out. The following set of instructions is uncomplicated and the easiest ones for a beginner spoon carver to learn as you will be using a technique similar to the Side-to-Side Cut (see pages 70–1).

For practising this cut, take a pre-hollowed-out circle from your Side-to-Side Cut practice. It will be much easier if the hollow has a good amount of depth – roughly 1cm (½ in.) – at the centre with a relaxed, gradual incline to its wall. Make sure that the hollow has been carved close to the end of the length of wood as this will make for a better grip when cutting.

The crisp curved line around the inside edge of the bowl is created by first carving around one half of the circular bowl and then followed by carving separately around the second half. You cannot sweep around the whole circular edge in one move. You might not be able to see it clearly yet, but this is another example of the uphill-downhill restriction when working with wood. Do not worry. After carving a few spoons, you will begin to get a feel for the language of wood grain.

With an indelible pencil, draw a horizontal line across the middle of the hollowed-out spoon bowl. Just as you did for the Pull Cut, hold the length of wood at one end in one hand and the crook knife in your other hand. Anchor the thumb of your knife-holding hand on the side of the wood just below the pencil line. Tilt the length of wood to roughly a 45 degree angle, so that your wood-holding hand is now angled higher than your knife-holding hand. Position the blade of the crook knife on the pencil line. This cut is achieved by simultaneously pulling and levering with your knife-holding hand – just as you did when making the Side-to-Side Cut – and by pivoting the wrist on your other hand so that the top end of the piece of wood swings towards you. Remember to keep your thumb anchored at all times. This allows the blade of the crook knife to make one continuous sweep

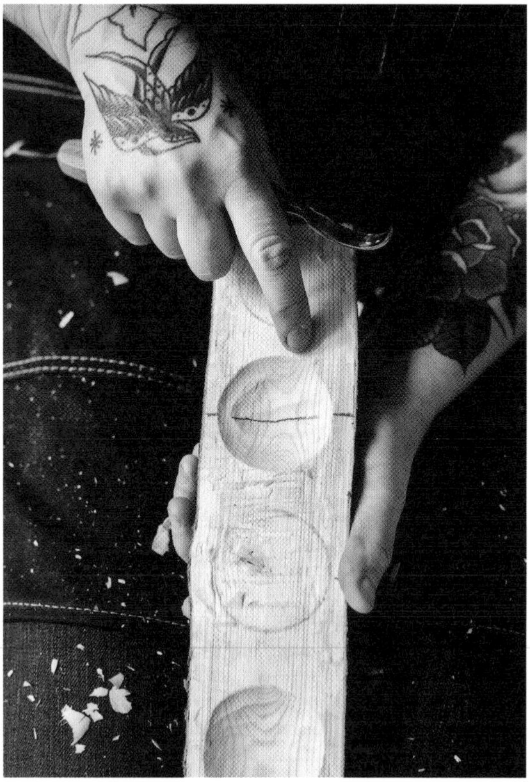

action all the way round the edge of the hollow and to the opposite side of the pencil line. Try miming the cut before you make it. Again, make sure that the cut finishes above the thumb on your knife-holding hand.

When you feel ready, go ahead and make the Curved Cut. You do not need to go too deep with this cut to achieve a crisp curved edge. Do not be tempted to sweep further past the pencil line; this cut works best when made in two halves. If you need to repeat the cut on the first half of the spoon bowl, keep your hands in position then swing and pivot back to the start of the pencil line and make the cut again.

Now make the Curved Cut on the second half of the spoon bowl. In the same way as you did for the Side-to-Side Cut, turn the length of wood around. Your knife-holding arm should now be crossing over your wood-holding arm. Tilt the length of wood at a 45 degree angle, position the blade where you stopped on the first cut and proceed to work around the curved edge in the same way. Similarly, as with the first half of the curve, while sweeping the cut around from one side to the other you should be able to achieve a pulling motion with the knife, but this time an outwards swinging motion with the wood. Practise making the two half curved cuts meet, then practise further until they appear to meet seamlessly. Later on you will be hollowing bowls into a piece of wood that is already at a spoon-shaped stage. Bear in mind that as the wood will be less chunky to hold by the point that you are refining the bowl of your spoon, so the Curved Cut will probably feel a little easier to execute.

When you have finished practising all the crook knife skills, carefully and gently wipe the blade with a dry cloth and store it safely.

YOUR NEWFOUND WOODWORKING SKILLS

If you put together all of the axe and knife skills that I have demonstrated over the preceding pages, you now have a decent set of foundation skills to kick-off your green wood carving. In the next section of this book, you will be using these newfound woodworking skills to make wooden utensils. Honing these skills will mean that you are not limited to making spoons alone. Of course, I want you to carve many spoons – I want the whole world to be carving spoons – but the wonderful thing about the axe, straight-edge knife, and crook knife skills that you have learnt is that they are transferable. Pair them with your imagination and you will be able to create all sorts of wooden treasures.

“

During a workshop, the spoon acts as the catalyst for the maker to tap into a creative well of energy deep within, to connect with the natural world in all its perfect imperfection, and to enjoy truly living in the moment.

”

PREPARING WOOD

Spending time carefully and correctly preparing a piece of wood, ready for carving, is a significant part of the spoon carving process and ultimately will greatly enhance the end results. This section presumes that you already have some freshly harvested green wood to work with, so make sure that you have read the section on where to find green wood and how to harvest it (see page 22). If you have used up all of your green wood supply practising your axe and knife skills, or the wood you have has gone a little bit too hard – or seasoned – to carve, then now would be a great time to go for a walk in the local woodland to gather some fallen branches or offer to help your neighbor prune the tree that you have been eyeing up since you started reading this book. We are going to start this section by making a tool that helps you to prepare wood for spoon carving. It is an essential bit of kit called a beetle mallet and it makes splitting logs a total breeze.

Making a Beetle Mallet

A beetle mallet is a very simple and often rather crude looking wooden implement. It is used in spoon carving to hit the back of the axe head when splitting a log. They are quite mean, yet comical looking objects and one of the first things students are amused by when they attend a spoon carving workshop.

The word 'Caveman' has been mentioned more than a few times when the beetle mallet is unpacked from my toolbox. I made my current beetle mallet from a hunk of beech about three years ago, when I started carving spoons full time. It has held up to some vigorous beatings during this period. Alas, it is now coming to the end of its life, but happy I will be as it goes into the wood burner this winter to keep the workshop warm while I make another one.

To make a beetle mallet, you need a branch, stem or trunk of tree of medium diameter (approximately 10cm or 4 in.) and that is roughly 40–60cm (15–25 in.) long. To transform this piece of wood into a beetle mallet, all you are going to do to is put a handle on it so that it is more comfortable to use.

This is where you get to practise your axe skills again in order to fashion a handle on your beetle mallet. Place one end of the length of wood onto the chopping block. Stand to one side of the chopping block (the opposite side to your axe-holding hand) and proceed to chop away – just as you did when first learning how to use your axe (see page 32). Some people like a long handle on their beetle mallet while others prefer a shorter one. You are making this beetle for you. Welcome to the world of making your own tools exactly to your preferred specification.

Give the beetle mallet a gradual transition from handle to head, while keeping the neck area chunky. You do not want the head of your beetle mallet to break off when you are putting it through its paces it the next section on preparing wood.

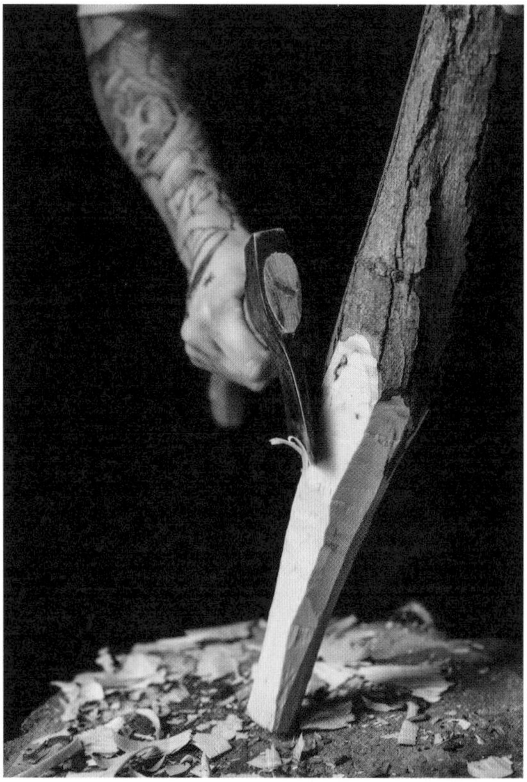

Splitting Wood

When splitting wood, everything is kept calm and controlled. There is no place for windmilling, lumberjack arms searing through the air. Equally, you do not need to be 'strong'. Woodworking is all about technique. I am going to show you two different techniques for splitting wood; the first for small- to medium-sized branch wood and the second for larger-sized log wood.

Study a piece of wood before you split it. Are there any knots? There probably are. Splitting wood is different from cutting and carving. When you split wood, the split follows the path of the wood grain so you want to check before you make the split that there are no knots, rot, or any strange occurrences laying across your intended split line. If there is a large enough knot in the way, your split is likely to travel around it, resulting in two uneven halves. Likewise, if there are visible nubs or areas where branches have been growing out, this will undoubtedly have some kind of grain-altering effect within your piece of wood (see below). You will not really know how much or how little an effect these natural occurences in the wood will have until you make the split, but there will inevitably be something to contend with.

SPLITTING BRANCH WOOD

This first technique is for splitting branch wood that is up to 5cm (2 in.) in diameter, so you do not need to use your beetle mallet just yet. As well as preparing green wood branches for spoon carving, this technique also makes a lovely job of splitting up dry, seasoned branches to use as kindling when building a campfire.

Start by taking a length of branch wood roughly 40cm (15 in.) long. While standing, hold the wood firmly at one end and place the other end on to the edge of your chopping block. Holding your axe near the end of its handle, place the blade onto the chopping-block end of the branch to be split. Make sure that the nose of the blade overlaps the end of the branch by about 1cm (½ in.). Now, you need to make your arms work together in tandem. Lift the branch a little way above the chopping block while also lifting the axe at the same time, making sure that the blade does not leave the surface of the branch. Bring the two back down together with a 'smack' onto the edge of the chopping block, making sure the axe finishes its cut onto the block (see overleaf).

If you have made the split successfully, your axe will have divided the branch through to the chopping block. If this is the case, stay in position and lever the axe gently to one side while levering the branch in the opposite direction. The split should carry on right the way down the length of the branch, separating it into two halves.

If you did not manage to make the split successfully with the first attempt, repeat the 'smack' action once more with the axe on the branch onto the edge of the chopping block. If the levering action to continue the split proves to be a little tough, carefully remove the axe head and pull the two halves apart with both hands.

GRÄNSFORS BRUK
SWEDEN

SPLITTING LOGS

Splitting logs in preparation for spoon carving is enjoyable but also quietly meditative. The technique shown here can also be used to split dry, seasoned firewood at home.

You will need a log of no more than 30cm (12 in.) in length that has been cut squarely on at least one of its ends, so that it stands up straight without support on your chopping block. Anything between 5cm–25cm (2–10 in.) diameter will be fine. For any branches of a smaller diameter, it is best to adopt the Splitting Branch Wood technique (see page 87). For any logs of a larger diameter, I recommend that you wait until you are a little more practised with the axe.

With your beetle mallet close to hand, stand the log in the centre of the chopping block. This time you need to hold the axe in your less dominant hand (the opposite hand to the one you write with). With consideration, place the axe blade directly on the place where you would like to make the cut. This is an opportunity to take a look for that tiny dot somewhere in the middle of the top surface of the log. This is the pith. If the pith is fairly central, take advantage of this and use the pith as your starting point for the axe cut and aim to split through it. This will make life a lot easier in the next section where we will be removing the pith altogether.

Hold the axe so that the axe head remains upright and square at all times. For your safety, once you have positioned the axe blade on the log, step a quarter of the way around the chopping block so that your entire body (except for your axe-holding arm) is now at a 90 degree angle to the axe handle. This is to ensure that the axe head has a clear pathway after it makes the split and will continue to swing through and out to the side. Remember to adopt this position whenever splitting logs in this way.

Keeping the axe in position, take hold of your beetle mallet and make a gentle, but confident, tap onto the back of the axe head. You will notice that even a light tap will have quite an impact. Savour this moment, before making a few more taps and enjoying the very satisfying feeling of the log cracking into two halves. With some practice, you will know how tough – or how gentle – you need to be to effect an efficient split with only three or four taps. Hopefully, you now have a log split into two halves, which could indeed make two spoons.

If your log was of quite a sizeable diameter to begin with then you will need to take one of those split halves and, using the same technique, split it again into quarters. Continue to repeat this process until you have a piece of wood with at least one face that is the desired width for your project. By now, you will be able to see that it is possible to make many lengths of wood from a single log. Many lengths of wood will make many spoons.

Remember, only split pieces of wood that you intend to use straightaway. Left whole, wood will stay fresher – or 'in the green' – for longer.

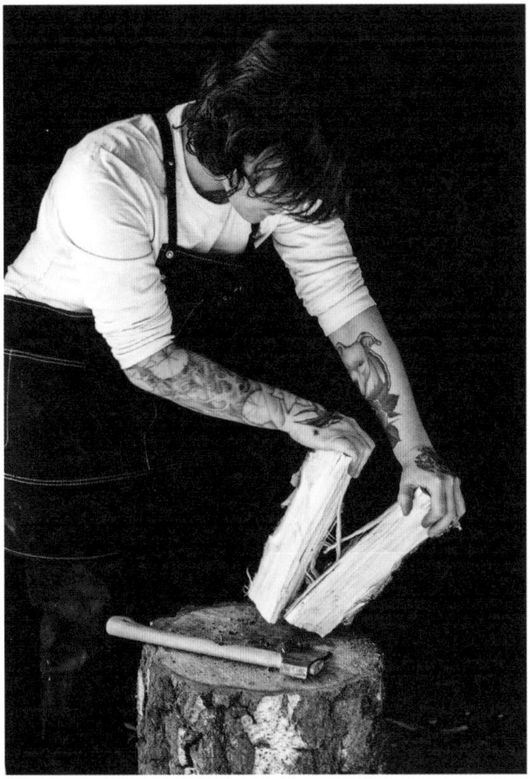

REMOVING PITH

No matter which method you used to split your wood, you will always need to remove the wood's pith. Every trunk, branch and twig of a tree has a pith running through its central core. If you used the pith to start your split then, for the most part, the pith should now be exposed and running vertically down the middle of each half of the wood. If you split a log into quarters, eighths, or more and you used the pith point to start those splits, then your pith will be now be running down the edge of a length.

The pith in some wood is very dark and bold while in others it is barely visible. As soon as a piece of wood is cut or split, it starts to dry out. The pith itself will begin to draw in all the moisture it can from the surrounding wood fibres to keep itself alive, resulting in dry, cracking, radial splits. Check your seasoned firewood at its ends for examples of radial splits. Simply put, if you carve a spoon from wood that has the pith left in, your spoon will end up with a crack in it.

Let's remove the pith now. Just as you did during axe practice, place the length of wood on the chopping block and use your axe to chop away the pith. Try not to gouge the pith out with the heel or toe of the axe; make sure you are using the whole blade to chop even, thin, business card-size slices from the wood's surface.

One benefit of this job is that you can flatten and smooth out the surface of the wood at the same time as removing the pith, ready for drawing a spoon design onto. Some lengths of wood will have quite a twist in them. I never get too caught up with trying to flatten out or correct this – ultimately, it adds charm, character and even more uniqueness to any spoon. Do not go too deep when removing the pith. Most piths only go a few millimetres deep into the wood and, if you chose a branch with a small diameter to work with, then you do not want to start chopping away at the limited amount of available 'spoon-wood'.

Once you have removed the pith, flattened and smoothed out the surface a little, you will be ready to draw your design onto the piece of wood and start making spoons.

Spoon Carving Projects

In this section of the book, I will show you how to carve a selection of different spoon designs using all the axe and knife skills you have learnt so far. There will also be some variations and advancements on those skills to try out along the way. The spoon designs I have chosen to include are the ones that I carve all the time; they are the designs most frequently requested. Do not get too caught up on making your spoons look exactly like the ones pictured in this book. By nature, they will not. For one thing, every piece of tree is different from the next.

Spatula

Okay, okay, I know what you are going to say. A spatula is not a spoon. No, it is not a spoon, but it is a great place to start when learning to carve. So just think of a spatula as a spoon without a bowl. They are so useful that I am sure you will end up making lots of these.

To make a spatula you will need a length of branch wood between roughly 30cm–35cm (12–14 in.) length and approximately 5cm–6cm (2–2½ in.) in diameter. Split and prepare the branch wood with your axe in the same way I showed you back in the Preparing Wood section (see pages 86–93). Once the wood is split, feel free to make two spatulas – one from each half of the branch. To keep things simple, the instructions that follow refer to using one half of a branch to make a single spatula.

After you have removed the pith and smoothed away the inside face of the wood's surface, turn the branch half around and chop away its rounded back side. Carve the plank to make it tapered – roughly 2cm (1 in.) thick at one end, gradually tapering down into 1cm (½ in.) thickness at the other end. Using an indelible pencil, draw a spatula shape onto one of the faces of the wood. Try to use as much of the piece of wood as possible. In other words, draw the side edges of the spatula head right up to the side edges of the wood and use the whole length of the piece of wood for the handle. At this stage in your carving journey, it would be advisable to draw some nice relaxed shoulders onto your spatula, transitioning gradually between head and handle with no sharp or acute angles.

Using your axe, carve around the spatula shape you have drawn. Holding the head end of your spatula, with the handle end resting on the chopping block, make some Release Cuts (see pages 42–5) all the way up one side of the handle to the neck of the spatula. Remove the wood by carving all the way back down to the bottom.

Using your axe, split and prepare the branch wood. Remove the pith, smooth the inside surface and chop away the back side to make a plank that is tapered towards one end.

Draw a spatula shape onto one of the faces of the wood, using the whole length of the wood and taking the edges of the spatula head right out to the sides of the wood.

Holding the head, carve the spatula shape following the pencil outline. Make release cuts along each side of the handle up to the neck of the spatula, then carve away the wood.

Turn the spatula around and then, holding the handle, roughly carve around the spatula head. Carve until you are within 1–2mm ($^1/_{16}$–$^1/_8$ in.) of the pencil outline.

Tilting the spatula at an angle, carve away the top straight edge of the spatula head. For a squared end, trim it with a saw. You now have a spatula blank.

Chop away more wood from the front and back faces of the spatula, maintaining the taper from the thicker handle down to the thinner spatula head.

Using your straight-edge knife, starting high up the neck and working down the handle, create smooth facets along the length with Pull Cuts and Planing Pull Cuts.

Carve away the wood up to the pencil lines using whichever cut, or combination of cuts, leaves the cleanest surface and keeps the taper even down the length of the handle.

Using a straight-edge knife, make Chest Expander or Potato Peeler Cuts to add a chiselled edge to the straight end of the spatula head on both the front and back faces.

Keep doing this until you are 1–2mm ($^{1}/_{16}$–$^{1}/_{8}$ in.) away from the pencil outline. Still holding the spatula head, turn the piece of wood around and remove wood down the other side of the handle. Now turn the piece of wood upside-down, so that you are holding the handle end and proceed to carve around the spatula head – again 1–2mm ($^{1}/_{16}$–$^{1}/_{8}$ in.) away from your pencil lines. Holding the spatula at an angle, carve away the top end of your spatula head. (If it is a squared end then you will need to trim it with a saw.) Congratulations. You have just made a spatula blank.

Now, using your straight-edge knife, start to smooth out the length of the spatula handle by using the Pull Cut method (see page 55). Begin the cuts up into the neck of the spatula, cutting down the length of the handle as far as you can go. Transform the Pull Cuts into Planing Pull Cuts (see pages 56–7). You could even turn the spatula around and try some Chest Expander Cuts (see pages 63–5). Use whichever of these cuts leaves the cleanest surface after cutting. Stop occasionally to check that you are keeping the taper even throughout the length of the spatula.

Once you have carved right up to the drawn pencil lines and the handle is looking nice and smooth, it is time to refine the head of the spatula. Work your way around the sides and both faces of the spatula head using Chest Expanding Cuts.

Lastly, you will want to add a chiselled edge to the end of the spatula head. You can either use a Chest Expander Cut or a Potato Peeler Cut (see pages 58–9) to achieve this. When you are happy with your refined spatula shape, finish off by adding a fine chamfer to any sharp or 'live' edges using a series of Pull Cuts, Planing Pull Cuts, Chest Expander Cuts or Potato Peeler Cuts where appropriate.

Using Chest Expander Cuts, refine the spatula head by working across both front and back faces to create a smooth surface. Work around the sides to neaten the spatula shape.

Using Chest Expander Cuts again, or alternatively Thumb Push Cuts, add a chamfered edge to the end of the spatula handle.

Lastly, neaten the very end of the spatula handle using a Potato Peeler Cut and then add chamfers to any other sharp, 'live' edges.

Cooking Spoon

Perhaps the most archetypal spoon of all time, the cooking spoon is so simple and yet the design variations are almost endless. For this project I am going to show you how to make an uncomplicated cooking spoon that is functional yet beautiful in its purity.

To make a cooking spoon you will need a length of branch wood about 30cm (12 in.) long and approximately 5cm–6cm (2–2½ in.) in diameter. Split and prepare your length of branch wood (see pages 87–93) then, using an indelible pencil, draw the outline of a cooking spoon on to one – or both – of the branch halves. As with the Spatula, draw some relaxed, sloping shoulders on this spoon and take the edges of the spoon head right out to the sides of the wood. In exactly the same way you did when making the Spatula, turn the wood around and, using the axe, chop away at the curved back side of the branch wood to create a small plank of wood of about 2cm (1 in.) even in thickness from top to bottom.

Chop away the wood either side of the pencil outline for the handle with your axe, starting from the sloped

neck area and working all the way down to the end of the handle. Use Release Cuts (see pages 42–5) to assist with this controlled carving all the way down the handle.

Once you have finished roughly shaping the handle, turn the piece of wood upside down so that the spoon head is resting on the chopping block, ready to roughly shape the back side of the spoon bowl. Starting just above the shoulders, on the back side of the spoon, chop three large facets: one straight facet in the middle of the spoon bowl and then one angled facet on either side of the first to create the basic foundations of a rounded spoon bowl. When chopping these facets on the back side of the spoon blank, it is easy to work beyond the drawn spoon outline on the front face. Do flip the spoon blank over to check that you have not gone too far with your carving. Likewise, you need to leave enough depth around the edge of the spoon to create a rim later on.

Now turn the spoon blank the other way up again so that the handle end is resting on the chopping block. Still working on the back side of the spoon, carve away some more wood from the handle. This time work on the diagonal lengths, from the neck all the way down to the handle end. Aim to create a spine-like shape. This will add strength and make your spoon unsnappable.

Stop and look at your spoon blank. Consider its shape, especially from the side. Does the transition between the head, neck and handle graduate smoothly? Are there any bumps or lumps? Or perhaps the neck area looks humped? If so, pick up your axe again and take some more wood off, working in the same cutting

Holding the head end and resting the handle end on the chopping block, use an axe to make a series of release cuts along each side of the handle up to the neck of the spoon.

Using the axe, chop down the length of the spoon following the pencil outline and the grain of the wood. Each time you hit a release cut, a section of wood will fall away.

Turn the spoon around and then, holding the handle, roughly carve around the spoon head. Carve until you are within 1–2mm ($^1/_{16}$–$^1/_8$ in.) of the pencil outline.

Turn the spoon around again and carve away more wood from the length of the handle until you are within 1–2mm ($^1/_{16}$–$^1/_8$ in.) of the pencil outline.

Resting the head end on the chopping block, roughly shape the back of the spoon bowl. Chop three large facets; one in the middle and then one angled on either side.

Once happy with the overall shape, refine the spoon with your straight-edge knife. Smooth the handle using pull cuts, planing pull cuts and anchored pull cuts.

Working on and around the previously axed-out facets, use a series of chest expander cuts to refine the back of the spoon bowl and add more roundedness.

Before hollowing out the bowl of the spoon, draw an inner circle in pencil onto the front face of the spoon head using a pair of compasses.

directions as before. Remember, if you are cutting in the wrong direction the cut will not feel easy and the wood edges will appear torn and fuzzy, as opposed to smooth and glassy.

Once you have a rough shape that you are happy with, you can start to refine the spoon with your straight-edge knife. To begin with, smooth out the length of the handle by using the Anchored Pull Cut method (see page 56), then switch to some Pull Cuts (see page 55) and perhaps eventually add some Planing Pull Cuts (see page 56) and Chest Expander Cuts (see pages 63–5). Start these cuts up in the neck of the spoon and extend them down the handle to achieve long, glassy facets all the way round the spoon handle.

Once you have carved up to the pencil lines and the handle is looking smooth, move on to refine the back side of the spoon bowl. Working on and around the three previously axed-out facets, use a series of small Chest Expander Cuts to add more shape and roundedness.

When you are satisfied with the overall shape of the spoon, it is time to hollow out the bowl. Using a pair of compasses, draw an inner circle onto the front face of the spoon head. Using a crook knife, hollow out the spoon bowl with Side-to-Side Cuts (see pages 70–3), Down Cuts (see pages 74–5) and Curved Cuts (see pages 76–9), remembering to work the area evenly and consistently until the spoon bowl has reached the required depth. Although a cooking spoon usually has quite a shallow bowl, it is up to you how deep you make it – after all, it is your cooking spoon. Do not forget to use your crook knife skills to sweep around the inner edges of the bowl to create a clean bowl edge.

Next, you will want to tidy up the top face of the bowl rim. Use some slow and controlled Pull Cuts and Chest Expander Cuts with the tip of your straight-edge knife. Finally, add chamfers to any sharp, 'live' edges, especially around the end of the spoon head where it will get bashed about inside the saucepan.

I recommend that you make three cooking spoons in succession, one immediately after the other. I promise that you will see a huge progression in your spoon carving skills from the first spoon to the third.

Continue to refine the contours of the spoon, working down the length of the handle and across the back of the bowl, until you are satisfied with the shape.

Working within the inner circle drawn onto the front face, hollow-out the spoon bowl by working side-to-side cuts, down cuts and curved cuts with a crook knife.

Neaten the top face by working around the rim of the bowl with the tip of a straight-edge knife. Use pull cuts and chest expander cuts. Add chamfers to any sharp, 'live' edges.

Using thumb push cuts and potato peeler cuts, neaten the end of the spoon handle by adding chamfers to the edges and cutting down the handle to your preferred length.

Hanging Jar Spoon

The perfect solution for spoons that persistently want to slide down the inside of tall jars, this long and slender jar spoon has the welcome addition of a small arm (see page 10). Once perched on the rim of a jar, your hanging jar spoon will stay in place and all will be well.

There are two ways to approach this project. The first is to scout about for the branch of a tree that has an offshoot branch growing out of it in a suitable position and angle. This is not a difficult task, after all, this is how trees grow. You then carve a spoon from this branch wood, just as you have done with the other projects, but encorporating the 'hook arm' branch into your design. Simple. In case you cannot find such a branch, I will demonstrate the second way: how to create the same hanging jar spoon using a section of wood that has been split from a log.

With this design, especially on your first attempts, it is worth drawing your pencil outlines onto the wood in an almost three-dimensional way. In other words, draw the outline of your hanging jar spoon in the same way as you have done for previous projects, but then draw some

guidelines on to the side of the wood as well to demarcate the side profile of the spoon and highlight where the hook arm will be carved in place.

Once you are happy with your design, using your saw, make a Release Cut (see pages 42–5) on either side of the hook arm following the pencil line. Next, use your axe to split the wood down to the Release Cuts. Mark with a pencil where this should be, if you need to. I make lots of marks that highlight things very obviously, but if you observe where the grain is running on your piece of wood, you will be able to tell where your split will end up.

Carefully place the axe blade on top of the handle end of the piece of wood. Making sure the axe blade is firmly registered on the surface of the wood, raise the wood and axe a little way off your chopping block and then lightly tap it back down with just enough force to split the wood down to the sawn Release Cut (see pages 87–9). Remember to make your hands work in tandem and carry out this task considerately and slowly.

Once you have successfully split out that section of wood, turn the spoon blank the other way up and chop carefully down to the other Release Cut to remove another section of the wood. Now the hook arm has been created, move on to profiling the outer shape of the spoon.

Using your axe, chop down the sides of the handle. You will not be able to carve right up into the shoulders of the spoon if they are square or acutely angled, but do not worry too much about that. Go as close as you can while remembering to cut safely at all times. Turn the spoon blank up the other way and, still using your axe,

carve around the outline of the spoon head before cutting some facets on the back of the bowl to add some roundedness (see page 107). The axe is too big a tool to process the hook arm any further, so from now on use a straight-edge knife to add shape and refine the spoon.

Using your straight-edge knife, create square or acutely angled shoulders where the spoon head meets the handle. Step one: place the head end of your spoon on your breast bone and using the Pull Cut method (see page 55), carve down the sides of the spoon handle as far as possible, cutting into the shoulder wood as you come to the end. Step two: turn the spoon around and, using an Anchored Pull Cut (see page 56), cut around the spoon's shoulders towards the neck. You will most likely need to go back and forth several times between these two steps to achieve the desired result.

To refine the back of the spoon bowl, using a combination of cuts. On the top half of the bowl, work Chest Expander Cuts (see pages 63–5) and Thumb Push Cuts (see page 62) heading outwards and downhill. On the bottom half of the bowl, use Anchored Pull Cuts heading inwards and downhill.

Use Anchored Pull Cuts and Pull Cuts to create a gradual transition between the head, shoulders, neck, and handle of the spoon. Take the tip of the straight-edge knife up into and under the hook arm and use small, shallow Pull Cuts to refine this area. Use Chest Expander Cuts and Thumb Push Cuts to refine the hook arm itself.

Once you have refined the overall spoon shape, carve the bowl. Draw the outline of the spoon bowl so that it follows either the shape of the outer edge or a simple circle or oval. It is up to you. Remember to add a fine, shallow chamfer to any live edges that remain.

If you do happen to find a suitable branch for the first way of approaching this project, cut the branch section so that the offshoot is 2.5cm (1 in.) or so from one end, then trim the offshoot itself back to 2.5cm (1 in.) long. Split the branch so the offshoot is left intact on the back side of one of the branch halves. Take this half and remove the pith, before drawing your spoon design.

Draw the outline of the spoon onto the wood, also marking the side profile to show the position of the hook arm. Using a saw, make relief cuts either side of the hook arm.

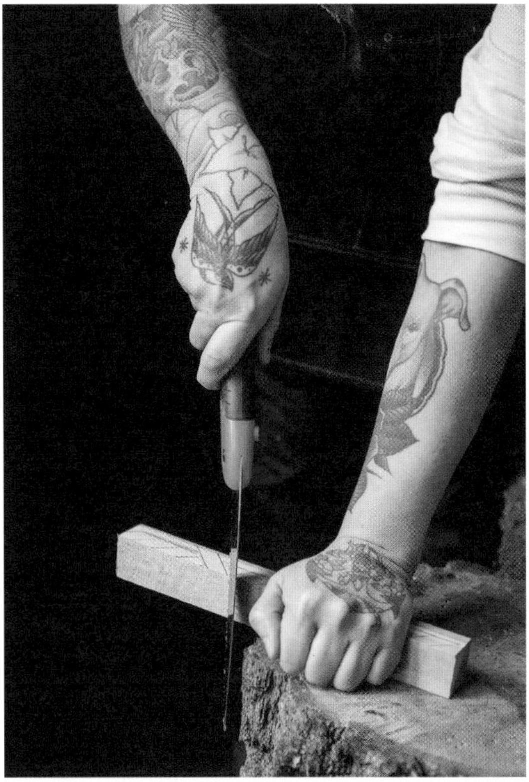

Using an axe, split along the grain of the wood from the handle end of the spoon blank down to the sawn release cut to remove the wood above the hook arm.

Turn the spoon blank the other way up, then chop down to the second sawn release cut to remove more wood and create the hook arm.

Using the axe, chop down the sides of the handle, around the head and across the back of the bowl to rough out the basic spoon shape.

Using a straight-edge knife, use the pull cut method to work down the sides of the handle and create long, smooth facets.

Use a combination of chest expander cuts and thumb push cuts to refine further the shape of the hook arm.

With the handle end of the spoon placed against your breastbone, work anchored pull cuts to shape the neck and shoulders.

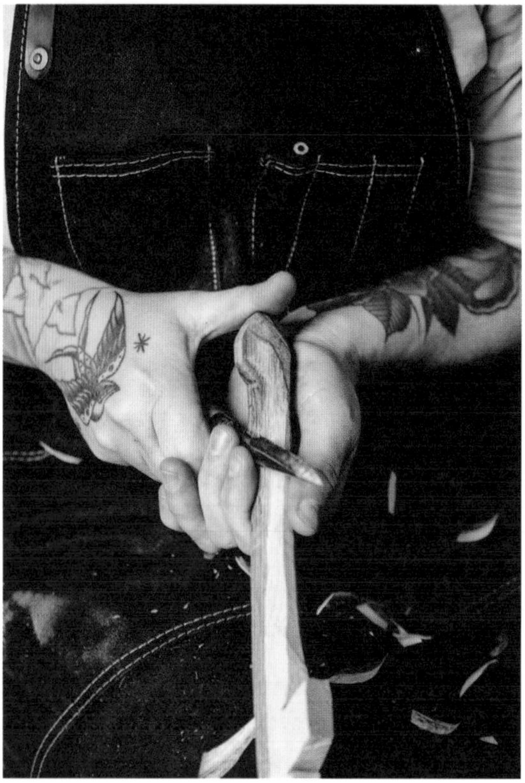

Refine the back side of the spoon bowl with chest expander cuts, thumb push cuts and anchored pull cuts.

Use anchored pull cuts and pull cuts to create gradual transitions between the spoon's head, shoulders, neck and handle.

Using a crook knife, hollow out the spoon bowl using side-to-side cuts, down cuts and curved cuts. Remember to chamfer any live edges.

Coffee Scoop

What defines this particular spoon as a 'scoop' is its deep bowl, which is capable of holding a measurement of coffee granules, tea leaves, powdered spices, or any other fine particles without spilling over the edge. Maybe you do not drink coffee, in which case feel free to rename this scoop accordingly.

To make a scoop, you will need a length of branch wood approximately 15–20cm (6–8 in.) long and 4–5cm (1½–2 in.) in diameter. The length of the handle will be cut shorter once the scoop is near to being finished as it is much easier to carve a spoon when you have more spoon to hold on to while working.

Split your length of branch wood and prepare it by removing the pith (see pages 87 and 92–3). Draw the outline of a scoop onto the cut face of the branch half. To achieve a precise circular head to the scoop, I use a pair of compasses to draw the outline.

Using your now developed and honed axe skills, chop and carve away at the branch half to create the scoop handle before turning it the other way up on your chopping block and carving around the top end of the

spoon bowl. The scoop has a much deeper bowl than the other spoon shapes we have been making, so do not axe too much off the back side of the bowl, otherwise you will lose the depth. Concentrate on carving a few steep angles to lift up the sides and the nose.

Once you are confident that your scoop blank is sufficiently roughed out and ready to refine, start working the handle with your straight-edge knife in order to create smooth and even facets. Create the back side of the rounded bowl; use Chest Expander Cuts (see pages 63–5) and Thumb Push Cuts (see page 62) heading outwards and downhill on the top half of the bowl. Use Anchored Pull Cuts (see page 56) to head inwards and downhill on the bottom half of the bowl. The more facets you add to the back side of the bowl, the rounder it will become. Keep checking and adding facets where roundedness is needed.

Opt either for relaxed sloping shoulders or the more angular ones used for the Hanging Jar Spoon. It is your choice. Use a combination of Pull Cuts and Anchored Pull Cuts (see pages 55–6) to create a smooth and gradual transition between the head, shoulders, neck and handle.

The scoop bowl is a deep one, so you will have to work a harder than you have on previous spoons to gain depth when hollowing out the bowl. Make sure you occasionally test the depth and walls for even thickness. You do not want to go too far with your scooping.

Finish your scoop by tidying up the rim, trimming down the handle to the desired length and adding a fine chamfer to any sharp, 'live' edges.

Split and prepare the branch wood, then draw the outline of the scoop on to the face of the wood. Using an axe, chop away wood up to the pencil line to create a spoon blank.

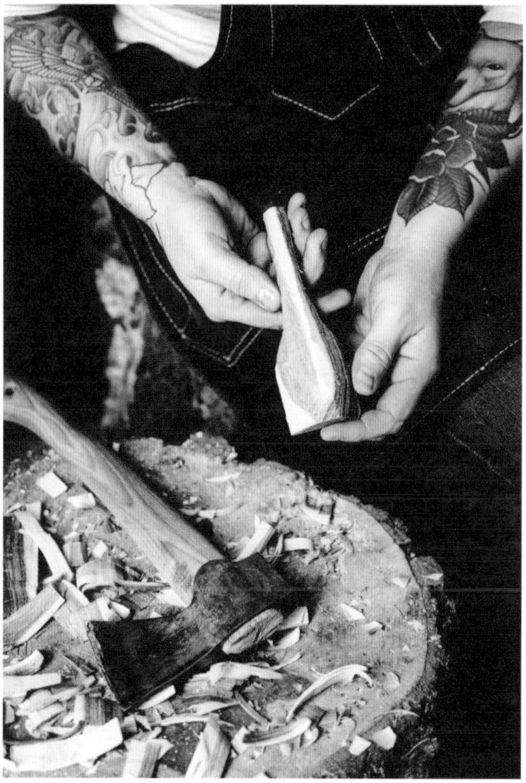

On the back side of the spoon, using an axe, carve steep angles and facets to create a deep bowl. Do not take off too much wood to retain the depth needed for the scoop.

Using a straight-edge knife, carve the handle into long, smooth and even facets by working a series of pull cuts, chest expander cuts and push cuts.

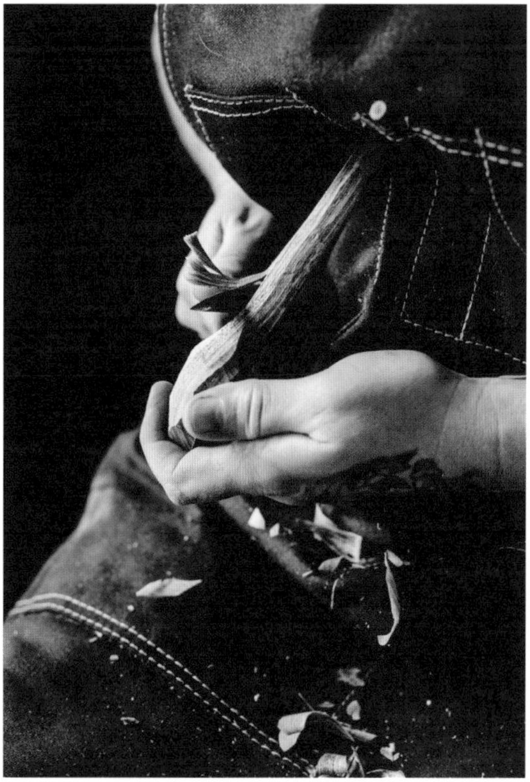

Working with the grain, add either relaxed sloping shoulders or sharper angular shoulders to transition between the bowl and the handle of the scoop.

Using a combination of chest expander cuts, thumb push cuts and anchored pull cuts, carve many small facets on to the back side of the bowl to add roundedness.

Before hollowing out the scoop bowl, tidy the spoon's edges and handle. For extra guidance, you can draw a second circle inside the bowl to mark the thickenss of the walls.

Using a crook knife, work a series of side-to-side and down cuts to hollow out a deep bowl. Regularly test the wall thickness and aim to keep it even throughout the bowl.

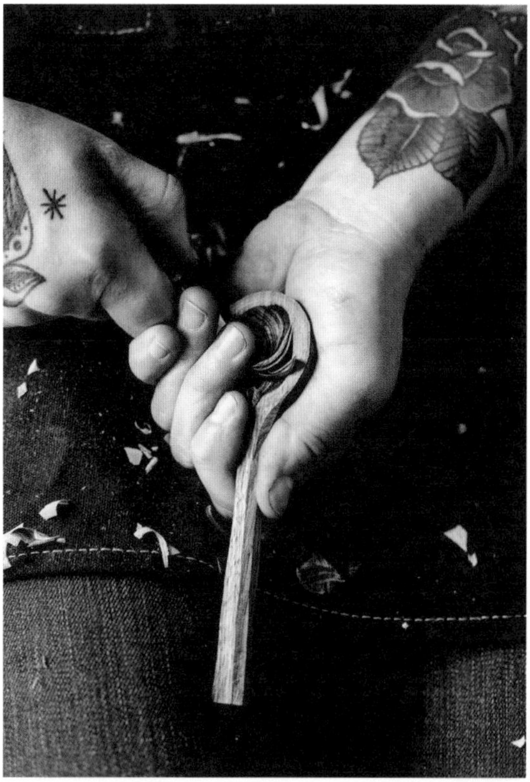

Using the straight-edge knife, tidy up the rim of the bowl, trim the handle down to the required length and add a fine chamfer to any sharp, 'live' edges.

Bent Branch Spoon

Hand carving a wooden spoon from the curved, crooked or bent branch of a tree is an exceptionally smart thing to do. Sure, you can shape a straight piece of wood into a curved spoon, but it will never look as elegant as a spoon carved from an already curved branch and nor will it have the same overall strength.

By looking at the wood grain lines that run vertically down the length of a spoon, you can tell whether or not a spoon has been made using a bent branch. When carved from a bent branch, these grain lines will follow the curved shape of the spoon from the top of the handle to the tip of the bowl (see page 31). There are many curved, crooked and bent branches out there and trying to find one is lots of fun. Sometimes I venture out on a bent branch hunt and, whenever I do find one, it feels as though I have struck arboreal gold.

For this project you will need a bent branch. The measurements of that branch are entirely your choice… or rather dependent on what you can find. Just to clarify, a bent branch is not a 'branch crotch'. A branch crotch is where one branch grows out from another branch, thereby creating a crotch or 'V' shape. A bent branch is a branch that has, for some reason, simply grown a bend somewhere along its length.

However long or wide your bent branch, you will certainly need to split the branch in half. Use the Splitting Branch Wood method (see page 87), this time tapping at one end to start a split before turning the branch around and tapping the other end to make another split. After making a split at both ends of the branch, you will be able either to pull apart the two halves or you will need to follow these initial splits in the wood with a few supplementary taps of the axe to divide the branch successfully into two halves. The wood fibres of the branch will follow the split – or the pull – leaving you with two bent branch halves. To finish preparing the

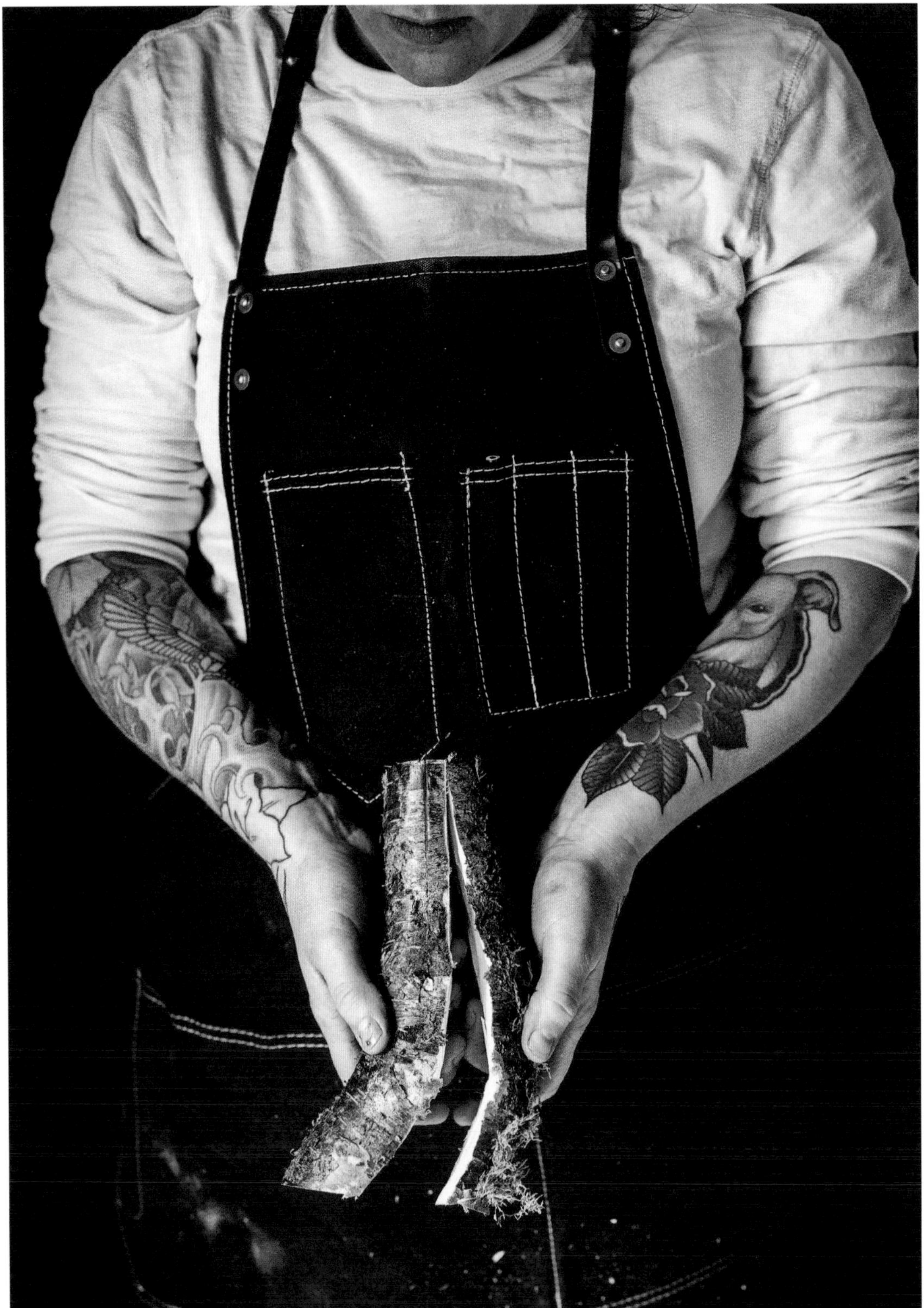

branch wood, using your axe, remove the pith that runs through the branch's core (see pages 92–3); chopping away the pith will prevent your spoon from drying out and ultimately cracking.

Next, using an indelible pencil, draw the outline of a spoon on to the face of the wood. Make sure the bowl of your spoon sits right in the crook or bend of the branch.

I always axe out my spoon handles first, but with a bent branch spoon any axing that follows will depend entirely on the type of bent branch you have, whether it is a dramatically crooked branch or has only a gently relaxed bend. Study the photographs of this bent branch spoon being carved (see overleaf). I am working with the axe, cutting in directions that I feel are the most effective and appropriate for this particular branch. This is where you get the chance to put all the skills you have learnt together, using your tools efficiently and reading the wood grain correctly, enabling you to axe out the bent branch spoon blank in the most suitable way.

Once you have finished carving the spoon blank with the axe, use the straight-edge knife to work around the spoon, shaping, smoothing and refining. This process is carried out in a very similar way to the previous spoon designs, except this time there is less of a strict order to follow. I usually carve a bit here and then a bit there to develop and refine continually the spoon shape.

Allow yourself to be directed by the natural properties of the branch wood; tune into the direction of the grain and carve the fibres in the way that feels most natural while adopting the usual grips, cuts and directions, before carving and hollowing out the bowl and them tidying up any sharp, 'live' edges.

Using your axe, split the branch wood into two halves by tapping each end to form a split and then pulling apart the two halves until the branch splits.

Draw the outline of your spoon onto the branch wood, making sure that bowl of the spoon sits in the bend of the branch, then axe away wood to create a spoon blank.

Turn the wood around and finish carving the spoon blank with your axe, chopping in whichever direction works best with the natural wood grain.

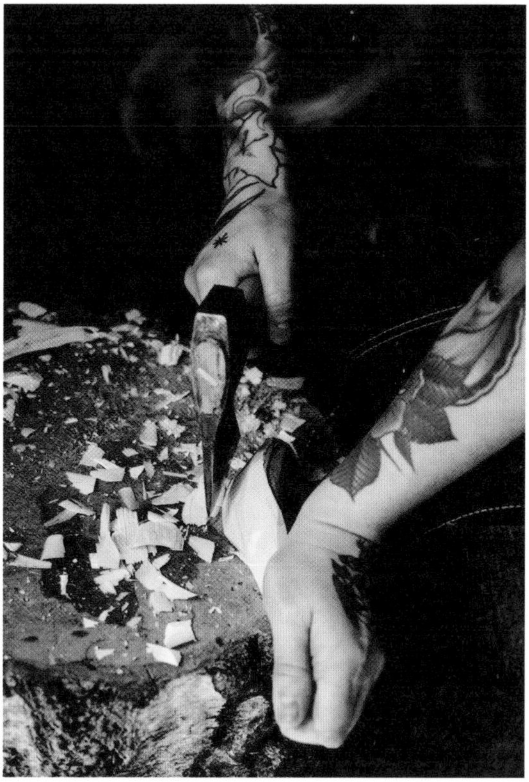

Reading the direction of the natural wood grain within the branch wood and using your axe correctly will create the most efficient cuts.

Using a straight-edge knife, shape the bowl, sides and handle of the spoon with a combination of pull cuts and planing pull cuts.

For the back side of the spoon, use a series thumb push cuts and chest expander cuts to create a rounded bowl.

Continue refining the shape of the spoon, using long pull cuts to carve along the length of the handle to create smooth facets.

Finally hollow out the spoon bowl with a crook knife, then tidy up any sharp, 'live' edges with the straight-edge knife.

Spoon Care

Because you have invested your time, energy, and love into carving them, wooden spoons are precious. However, nothing saddens me more than seeing a wooden spoon reduced to a purely decoative item hanging on the wall. Do keep in mind that a carved wooden spoon is best respected when it is used to cook and eat with.

Wooden spoons start to look their best after several weeks of stirring sauces, poking stir-fries, and flipping ingredients in oily pans, so do not hold back. Cook and eat delicious food with your spoons and soon a wonderful patina will develop, enhancing and enriching the natural colours and patterns within the wood.

A spoon does not need to season or dry after carving, so start using it straight away. You can even – shock, horror – pass them through the dishwasher to clean them.

If you want to give a spoon as a present, you might like to give it a little rub with some homemade spoon balm to make it look its very best.

SPOON BALM

200ml (7 fl. oz.) raw linseed oil
50g (2 oz.) solid beeswax (half of a bar)
Glass jar with a lid

Pour the raw linseed oil into a saucepan and place over a medium heat. Slowly warm the oil until hot, but do not allow it to boil. Chop the beeswax into small chunks and add it to the hot oil in the pan. Stir until the beeswax has completely melted. Pour the spoon balm mixture into a clean glass jar and allow to cool until it solidifies. Screw the lid onto the jar to keep the spoon balm dust free. Store at room temperature, the balm will keep for years.

To treat a wooden spoon, using a lint-free cloth, rub a small, pea-sized blob of balm into a completely dry spoon. Leave for a few moment, then using the cloth, wipe away any excess balm from the surface of the spoon that has not been absorbed into the wood.

Index

AFTERWORD

I hope you have found this book to be both informative and enjoyable. I have really loved writing it and I am so grateful to have been given the opportunity. For me, there is nothing more rewarding than being able to pass on these spoon carving skills. But working your way through this book is by no means the end of your learning. Spoon carving is a life-long journey to travel along: amassing knowledge about all the different tree species and the properties of their woods, honing your new set of basic woodworking skills and adding to them by learning some new or adapted cuts along the way.

Enjoy the ride. And do not forget to hug a tree every now and then or, at the very least, give them a little tickle as you walk by.

EJ

I would like to thank the following people for all their support on my personal spoon carving journey: Anne-Marie Osborne and Orla Osborne, for filling my world with love and allowing me to fill theirs with trees, spoons, and wood shavings. Marie Forsberg, for all the beautiful photographs in this book. Nick Tait, for food, laughter, and spoons… not necessarily in that order. Anthony Oram, (Evil) Gordon Stovin, LJ Hopkinson, and spoon carving students both past and present, I know some of you have continued to make spoons… I am delighted. The spoon carving community the world over for your constant inspiration. My lovely guests at 'A Weekend In The Woods', through rain and shine. My social media family, for all the follows, likes, and love. Polo, my four-legged best friend, for accompanying me on our many adventures into the woods and beyond. Thanks also to: Lisa Pendreigh and the team at Quadrille Publishing, Robin Wood, Bush Farm, Somerset, AOP, BeerBods, Break Fluid Coffee, The Heritage Crafts Association, TEDxBrighton, Interesting, Timbers, Thelma, Moore, Tictail, Hot Smokey Bastard Sauce, and Frome in Somerset – an amazing town, full of great people who are making wonderful things happen.

Publishing Director : Sarah Lavelle
Commissioning Editor : Lisa Pendreigh
Editorial Assistant : Harriet Butt
Creative Director : Helen Lewis
Design Direction : Charlotte Heal Design
Photographer : Marte Marie Forsberg
Production Director : Vincent Smith
Production Controller : Emily Noto

First published in 2017 by
Quadrille Publishing Ltd
Pentagon House
52–54 Southwark Street
London SE1 1UN
www.quadrille.co.uk

Quadrille is an imprint of Hardie Grant
www.hardiegrant.com.au

British Library Cataloguing-In-Publication Data
A catalogue record for this book is available from the British Library.

ISBN 978 184949 719 0

10 9 8 7 6 5 4 3 2 1

Printed in China.